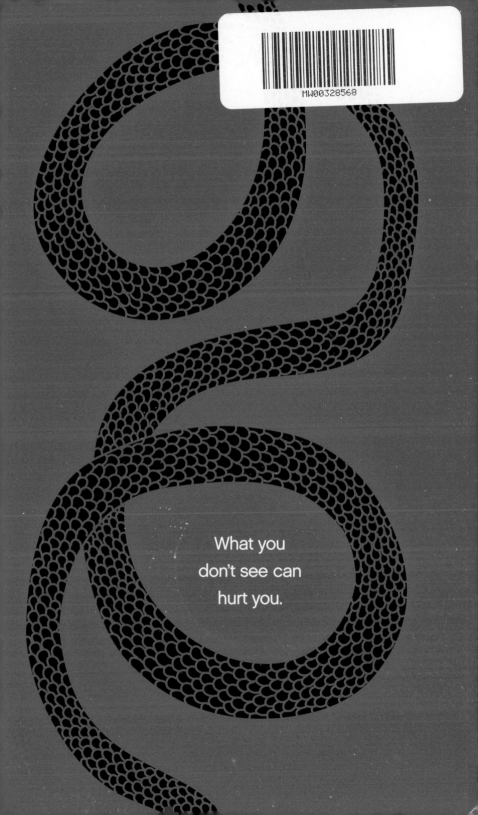

What you
don't see can
hurt you.

"One of the greatest gifts God has given to humans is the capacity for self-knowledge. We can navel-gaze into our own being like no animal ever dreamed. The capacity for self-awareness is both a blessing and a curse. If we are open to our blind spots, it is a blessing. If we deceive ourselves regarding who we are, it is a curse. Tim and Fil are working from the blessing side. Go with them."

Dan Boone, President, Trevecca Nazarene University

"It will take courage to read this book. It's uncomfortable to consider weakness. I'd much rather live in denial. In *Blind Spots*, Tim and Fil offer groundbreaking insights and help in not only identifying what you cannot see—but also finding freedom to move toward the person you want to be."

Tim Stevens, Vice President of Consulting, Vanderbloemen; author of *Marked by Love: A Dare to Walk Away from Judgment and Hypocrisy*

"Reading Tim and Fil's book feels like a conversation with a trusted friend. You can hear the tones of their caring voices in the stories they tell because they're stories they've lived. You can sense their profound wisdom as they bring Scripture to life because they have been transformed by God's Word. And somehow, while revealing the ugly realities of our blind spots, and telling us the truth that is hard to hear, their words make their readers feel known and loved. Read it and be changed."

Drew Hill, Pastor; author of *Alongside: Loving Teenagers with the Gospel*

"Jesus says that when we can see things clearly, our whole life will be full of light. That's precisely where Fil Anderson and Tim Riddle plunge into our smudged existence to help. With hard-won insight, they bring focus and clarity to critical matters that our hurry, self-deception, and pure thoughtlessness often turn to a muddled blur. In helping us attend to what we often miss, *Blind Spots* offers a gift as precious as sight."

Jedd Medefind, President, Christian Alliance for Orphans

"Only the most brazen and foolish presume they are fully self-aware. Most mere mortals know there are countless ways we fail to see what we need to know about ourselves. But how do you know what you can't see? Blind spots are a problem that leave us knowing we are significantly near or farsighted without the glasses to correct our vision. Tim Riddle and Fil Anderson have written a compelling and honest book that offers light to fill the spaces we can't see. What we can't see can kill us or our jobs, marriages, and friendships, but when we learn to see, it opens our eyes to wonder about how Jesus pursues us even in the midst of our refusal to see. *Blind Spots* is a brilliant gift to anyone who longs to let the truth set them free."

Dan B. Allender, Christian therapist; author; speaker focusing on sexual abuse and trauma recovery; professor of counseling psychology; founding president of The Seattle School of Theology and Psychology

"*Blind Spots* is a short and wonderfully narrative take on our pervasive lack of self-clarity. Practical and personal stories provide a lens to open our eyes to things others see about us that we miss. I think of how Jesus told his disciples at the Last Supper, 'I have many things to say to you that you cannot yet bear. But when the Spirit of Truth comes, he will lead you into all truth.' I am so grateful that this book gives the opportunity to bear more truth and see ourselves anew. Reading *Blind Spots* was Jesus's invitation to address blind spots that sabotage my relationships. It gave efficient ways to participate with God's Spirit in responding to truth about myself."

Adele Calhoun, Pastor of Spiritual Formation, Highrock Covenant Church; author; spiritual director; retreat leader; pilgrimage leader; certified Enneagram instructor

"The very thought that there is something unseen in me that hinders my intimacy with Jesus, or deters my true self from emerging, is what compels me to read *Blind Spots*. The insight, challenge, and practical help offered, combined with the Holy Spirit's work within, revealed several of my personal 'blind spots' to keep exploring. Thank you, Fil and Tim."

Ty Saltzgiver, Author of *My First 30 Quiet Times* and numerous other titles; husband; father; speaker; mentor

"Did you know there is a difference between looking and seeing? So many of us spend lots of time looking without ever really seeing. In *Blind Spots*, Tim and Fil take an honest and profoundly authentic look at some of the places that keep us blind, groping in the dark. Bringing light to dark places, Tim and Fil not only expose our blind spots but help us move toward truth, freedom, boldness, and strength. A must-read!"

John Wagner, Young Life SVP Global Cities; author of *Perfect: Sacred Stories from the Heart of a Dad*

"It's often said that 'seeing is believing.' However, in *Blind Spots*, I learned just the opposite—that believing is seeing. That regarding the things we can't see about ourselves, we only develop twenty-twenty vision when we've been lovingly seen by a chosen few and by the One whose gaze of affection and acceptance sets us free. After reading this treasure of a book written by Tim Riddle and Fil Anderson, I finally understand why St. Paul asked God to 'open the eyes of our hearts.'"

Michael John Cusick, Author of *Surfing for God*; CEO at Restoring the Soul

"In these pages, you'll find the authors diligently and honestly trying to uncover and address a crucial topic. In so doing, they successfully offer a helpful start to the lifelong and freeing practice of journeying with God to discover, reveal, and attend to reality. Many will find this book to be a great help. Your loved ones will be glad you read it."

Nathan Foster, Director of Community Life, Renovaré; author of *The Making of an Ordinary Saint*

"*Blind Spots* is so much more than just a book. It is a mirror through which we can see our souls. With truth and grace, the authors hold up this mirror for us to take a deep look at what needs to be addressed in our own lives. I wish I had read this book decades ago. I'd be a better man, and now I have that invitation to become a better version of myself and you do too! Sometimes the truth can be too hard to accept. But in this book, we find that the truth sets us free. By first knowing our blind spots, then having them brought to the light, we can see our way more clearly to walk with confidence into the future to experience all God has for us."

Stephen W. Smith, President and Spiritual Director of Potter's Inn; author of *The Lazarus Life* and *Soul Custody*

"In my forty years of being a pastor, it would have been so instructive and helpful to have this book. As it has been said, 'Sin blinds, it binds, and it grinds.' We all need a different set of eyes to see what we are missing. This book helps leaders to pay attention to the necessary internal work leaders need to do to serve and love their communities faithfully. Tim and Fil illustrate a critical topic for healthy, wholehearted leadership and share their stories with insight and wisdom."

Clyde L. Godwin, Director for The Barnabas Center Triad

BLIND SPOTS

BLIND SPOTS

WHAT YOU DON'T SEE CAN HURT YOU

Tim Riddle & Fil Anderson

New
Growth
Press

WWW.NEWGROWTHPRESS.COM

New Growth Press, Greensboro, NC 27404
www.newgrowthpress.com
Copyright © 2019 by Tim Riddle and Fil Anderson

Unless otherwise noted, Scripture quotations are taken from *The
Holy Bible*, New Living Translation, copyright © 1996, 2004, 2015
by Tyndale House Foundation. Used by permission of Tyndale House
Publishers, Inc., Carol Stream, Illinois 60188. All rights reserved.
Scripture quotations marked ESV are taken from The Holy Bible,
English Standard Version.® Copyright © 2000; 2001 by Crossway
Bibles, a division of Good News Publishers. Used by permission. All
rights reserved.
Scripture quotations marked NIV are taken from The Holy
Bible, New International Version®, NIV® Copyright ©1973, 1978,
1984, 2011 by Biblica, Inc.® Used by permission. All rights reserved
worldwide.
Scripture quotations marked NKJV are taken from the New King
James Version®. Copyright © 1982 by Thomas Nelson. Used by per-
mission. All rights reserved.
Scripture quotations marked CEV are taken from the Contempo-
rary English Version. Copyright © 1995 by American Bible Society.
Used by permission. All rights reserved.
Scripture quotations marked MSG are taken from The Message
(MSG) Copyright © 1993, 1994, 1995, 1996, 2000, 2001, 2002 by
Eugene H. Peterson. Used by permission of Tyndale House Publish-
ers, Inc. All rights reserved.

Cover Design: Faceout Books, faceoutstudio.com
Interior Typesetting and eBook: Lisa Parnell, lparnell.com

ISBN: 978-1-948130-59-2 (Print)
ISBN: 978-1-948130-60-8 (eBook)

Library of Congress Cataloging-in-Publication Data on File

Printed in South Korea

26 25 24 23 22 21 20 19   1 2 3 4 5

Contents

Dedication

(Tim)

To my wife, Stacy.
You've been my rock for thirty-three years.
You have loved me well and been incredibly supportive
throughout our journey together. Thanks for being my first
eyes and proofreader with every chapter I completed.
Your encouragement always motivated me to keep writing.
I love you dearly!

To my children; Ragan, Carly, Fletcher, and Ellie.
What a blessing! Thanks for being excited for me when I first
shared the idea and thanks for your encouragement and
confidence that I could do this, with God's help of course!
I love you more than you know!

To Harold and Ella Riddle, my mom and dad.
You left this earth way too soon but oh how you influenced me
well for thirty-one years. You provided the foundation for who I
am today, and you instilled the confidence in me never to stop
pursuing my dreams as long as God was leading the way!

(Fil)

To Lucie, my soul mate and best friend,
who knows me intimately, loves me regardless,
and is willing to be completely honest with me
about my blind spots.

Foreword

My father sold used cars. Consequently, we rode in all kinds of automotive makes and models during my childhood. I vividly recall my father's emphasis upon checking his blind spot. Since the cars were always shifting, so were the blind spots. A sporty fastback might obscure his vision much more than a big, wide station wagon. Sometimes a few adjustments in a rear-view mirror were sufficient. At other times, he needed our assistance, another set of eyes in the backseat to know it was safe to proceed.

Tim Riddle and Fil Anderson offer both the mirrors and the eyes we need to identify our blind spots. What we don't see can definitely hurt us—professionally, interpersonally, and in our spirit. The prophet Jeremiah admonished those "who have eyes and see not, and who have ears and hear not" (Jeremiah 5:21 NKJV). Ezekiel described a rebellious house "which has eyes to see but does not see" (Ezekiel 12:2 NKJV). Jesus hearkened back to the words of Isaiah, decrying a people who have grown dull; "their ears are hard of hearing, and their eyes they have closed" (Matthew 13:15 NKJV). This book considers the cost of such blind spots.

Clarity of vision is a prerequisite for long-term discipleship. How do we become those who Jesus describes as "blessed are your eyes for they see, and your ears for they hear" (Matthew 13:16 NKJV)? I am grateful to Tim and Fil for leaning into biblical stories of healing, where scales fall from a blind man's eyes. Fil and Tim communicate how much we need each other to root out our blind spots, to provide a corrective mirror. They also confess their own shortcomings, acknowledging their blind spots, calling us all to self-examination.

This book snapped me back to painful moments of revelation over thirty years ago. I was among a small group of students at Davidson College who volunteered to be part of an exercise during Reverend Charles King's seminar on racial reconciliation. I had plenty of African-American friends, so I felt confident I could display my understanding on racial justice issues. During the exercise, I found my hackles rising. He seemed to be treating some people in the circle differently than others, listening thoughtfully to some group members and brusquely cutting others short. My frustration rose. I pointed out the inequity in how he was treating some of us. He appeared indifferent, even blaming me for raising objections and causing problems. I completely lost whatever cool I'd brought into the circle.

Only then did Dr. King reveal his ruse. He'd set up social rules that worked against Caucasians. In his circle, the social construct favored black people over white people. And in just fifteen minutes, I was ready to rebel, primed for a battle, raging against injustice. How might a lifetime of inequality feel? How much rage would boil within students who had been judged, demeaned, shut down because of the color of the skin rather than the content of their character? Never before had I really stepped into African-American shoes. Suddenly, I understood a little better. My blind spot had been revealed, in public. I was far weaker than I imagined. More prone to anger than I'd guessed. And blind to the cost of racism, how it robs people of dignity and self-worth. Some blind spots are personal. Others are cultural. All include hidden costs. What else lurks beneath the surface, smoothed over when things go well but poised towards self-destruction or pointing fingers when circumstances change?

Tim and Fil invite us into a long-term project, discipleship rooted in deep heart work. Given how enmity trumps empathy in our public discourse, now is the time to examine our blind spots. Can we pause to identify the log in our own eye before pointing out the speck in our brothers and sisters? How great that Tim and Fil provide such honest correction for each other. They invite us into their wise and trustworthy process. How grateful I am for their encouragement to consider our own blindness. How else will we mature in faith and character? It is far too easy to sleep walk through life, seeing but not recognizing, listening but not truly hearing. A revelatory wake-up can arrive via Scripture, a sermon, a look, a hug, a movie, a song, or a book like this. *Blind Spots* is an opportunity for God to love us boldly, for Jesus to confront us gently, for the Spirit to sharpen our sight.

Enjoy the refining journey!

Craig Detweiler
President, The Seattle School
    of Theology and Psychology
November 2018

Acknowledgments

(Tim)

Thanks to my team at SMC; Suzanne, Connie, Tyler, Jessica, Karen, and Rena (TT). I still remember the day I shared with all of you that Fil and I were writing a book together. The smiles on your faces and your excitement meant more to me than you know. Thanks to the leadership of SMC for allowing me the freedom to write when I needed those blocks of time. Thanks to SMC for shaping my leadership over the past fourteen years which influenced the writing of this book. Thanks to Joanne Soliday, my friend and Bible teaching partner. You were the first person I talked to about the possibility of writing. We have dreamed a lot together over the years. Thanks to Adam Tarwacki. There are some relationships that life would not be the same without. When I decided to start a new chapter in my life, Discover Blind Spots, you said, "I will do whatever I can to help you." For that, I will always be grateful. Thanks for your friendship over these years.

Thanks to my writing partner Fil Anderson. You have been my spiritual mentor for many years now. I still remember the day I walked into your office and said: "Tell me about writing." Then you prayed that prayer and the rest is history! You have encouraged me more than you know. I could not have done it without you. Thanks for mentoring me throughout this process. Also, thanks for being my blind spot accountability partner and for showing me what it truly looks like to love Jesus!

(Fil)

I don't know who said it first, but I'm sure it's true: *If you ever see a turtle on a fence post, you can know it had some help getting there.* In other words, we don't accomplish anything in life alone. That's certainly been my experience co-authoring this book.

This book *Blind Spots* was Tim Riddle's original idea and an excellent one, at that. Thank you, Tim, for inviting me to join you in this rigorous, life-giving endeavor. I cherish your friendship and trust.

Thank you, New Growth Press, for believing in our message enough to invest your valuable resources into the publication of this book. Thank you especially for providing us with the outstanding assistance provided by Barbara Juliani, Ruth Castle, and Sue Lutz.

Thank you to Craig Detweiler for his eloquent foreword and other people, for whom my admiration is immense, who were willing to read our manuscript and offer their generous words of endorsement.

Whatever else remains a blind spot, one thing I see clearly: my contributions to this book were not mine alone. The insights and inspiration of many writers, teachers, and friends are so integral that, except for a few personal experiences I've cited, countless people have contributed to its writing. That notwithstanding, I'd like to thank the following people especially.

I am profoundly grateful for the Board of Directors of my ministry platform, Journey Resources, for their relentless devotion and confidence in me. Also, the many individuals who have faithfully and generously partnered with me as I do everything I can to offer the message of God's unconditional and limitless love for all people everywhere.

Thank you to the extraordinary pastoral team (Bob, Ben, Angela, Jeromy, Nick, and Jarm), staff, leadership, and members of St. Mark's Church, Burlington, NC, for encouraging me by your example, strengthening me by your prayers, and granting me the privilege of serving as your spiritual formation pastor.

Thank you, Mike and Susie, Bill and Joann, Steve and Robin, and Johnny (Sue, now deceased), for doing life together, so faithfully, with Lucie and me. You've provided a safe place to shed our tears, express our disappointments, expose our failures, and celebrate our joys.

Thank you, Notorious Sinners (you know who you are), for rivaling all others in the ways you have exposed your blind spots and helped me to see more of my own. The same goes to you, Mike Fowler and Rod Mortenson.

Thank you, Reality Ministries, North Street Community, and Corner House family for the ways you reflect God's compassionate heart for humanity by creating spaces with no margins where everyone is accepted, valued, and celebrated. You've uniquely assisted me in seeing priceless things that I've been blind to for most of my life.

Thank you, Mom, Linda, Steve, and Susan, for loving me unconditionally, through every stage of my life, despite my many blind spots.

God said, "A man's greatest treasure is his wife, she is a gift from the LORD" (Proverbs 18:22 CEV). Thank you, Lucie, for being my greatest treasure. Thank you, Lord, for the gift.

The three greatest treasures my life with Lucie has produced are our children. They are my greatest heroes. Our daughter has one of the most courageous yet most tender hearts I've ever known. I admire her compassion. I love you, Meredith, and I love Gabe, who wisely sees you as his greatest treasure. Corinne, you are precious, and I love you too. Our son Will is bright and devoted to living his life fully with integrity. I admire his determination. I love you, Will, and I love Katie, who is your greatest treasure. Collins, you are precious, and I love you too. Our son Lee relentlessly desires to generously and selflessly give his life away. I admire his sense of justice and compassionate love for others, especially those on the fringes. I love you, Lee.

A few thoughts before you begin reading

Recently I posted a question on one of my social media accounts:

"Are blind spots always blind . . . or do we try to hide them for our convenience at times?"

Little did I know it would spark a debate about the actual definition of blind spots. One friend posted in response:

"Blind spots by definition are blind. If you can see them, you can call them 'denial' spots but not blind spots."

Later he acknowledged he was merely busting my chops a little and he understood my point.

Shortly after our first edits of this book, our publisher suggested that we clearly explain our definition of blind spots because, as you will see as you read, our understanding is more broad than narrow.

Some wanted us to classify all blind spots as sins, and many are. But I (Tim) can provide examples of blind spots in my life that weren't the result of a sinful character flaw (although many others were). For that reason, to

1

be honest, we didn't want this book to focus only on how sinful we all are.

Here's an example. I love to speak and teach, but that gift was not revealed until about fifteen years ago. I had no idea it was something God wanted me to pursue. But through my spiritual journey and the encouragement of others, I realized it was something he was calling me to do. I don't think that blind spot was the result of sin! I think it was something that God was waiting to reveal at the right time in my life. However, if you had told me twenty years ago that I would be giving hundreds of talks to multiple audiences, I would have denied the possibility. At the time it was simply a blind spot.

So, let's get back to the idea of sin. I agree that a lot of our blind spots are rooted in our depravity and sinfulness. But are they really blind, or have we pushed them to the corners of our soul as an attempt to hide them? And who are we hiding them from: ourselves or others?

This leads me back to my friend's response to my social media post. Should we call them "denial" spots instead of blind spots? My friend suggested that most blind spots hang out in our shadows. They aren't completely invisible, but are still hard to see at times.

By now, you are probably thinking, "Is he going to define it or not?"

Fil and I had a long conversation about the definition one afternoon after a meeting with our editor. It has caused both of us to dig a little to affirm and defend the definition of "blind spots" in our book.

We finally decided that a blind spot (to us) is anything that stands in the way of being all that God has intended for our lives. Yes, many of those blind spots are sins, but others are rooted in ignorance, immaturity, circumstances, and sometimes the sins of others against us.

Sometimes, as with my speaking gifts, they are things we don't see because God has not yet revealed them to us. But blind spots of many kinds may fuel our fears of stepping out in faith to use the talents and gifts God has given us.

I found this definition of sin in the *Holman Illustrated Bible Dictionary*: "Actions by which humans rebel against God and miss His purpose for their life."

In the end, you will have to come to your own conclusion. Here's one thing Fil and I are confident about: Blind spots are real and can cause a lifetime of pain, anguish, and second guesses. Blind spots can keep you from being all that God has wired you up to be. What you don't see can genuinely hurt you, but thankfully we have a Savior who can help us identify our blind spots, forgive our sins, and give us the power and desire to see our blind spots removed. We hope that reading this book will reveal that truth more than anything else!

CHAPTER 1

How the Journey Began

Most Christians, I am afraid, are self-conscious but
not self-aware. — Peter Scazzero, *The Emotionally
Healthy Church*

(Tim)
As I sat there, I was stunned. I couldn't believe what I
was hearing. How could something manifest itself so
deep inside of me that it came out in words that still, to
this day, I can't remember saying? Could I actually have a
blind spot? Certainly not me, the most self-aware person
I know—or so at least I thought! I had spent most of my
adult life identifying blind spots in others and was completely blind to my own.

Entrepreneurial Blind Spots

I was thirty-one years old when I decided to start my
own business. I was young, energetic, and hard-working.
I also loved people. The prospect of assembling a team to
accomplish a meaningful goal was exciting to consider.

The new adventure began with just one employee: me.
I was the CEO and CFO, while also managing sales, the

warehouse, customer service, and shipping. In my spare time, I was the custodian and deliveryman. I quickly learned that wearing multiple hats was required in a start-up company. I also learned that long hours were a "hidden benefit" of ownership. But I loved every minute! Soon I was dreaming about hiring additional team members. The company was rapidly growing, and financially we were ahead of schedule. After five years, we had placed ninety highly skilled individuals onto multiple teams. My dream had finally come true. Or had it?

We began with a great idea, at an ideal time, with sufficient startup capital. We also were determined that our company would be an exceptional place to work. To keep our employees happy and productive, we offered frequent and open communication, regular recognition of achievements, and constructive feedback. Having these bases covered, I naively assumed that management would be easy.

Then along came John. He was a true professional who had gained excellent experience working with a larger company. Nonetheless, I quickly learned that John was disorganized, and his mess led to stress that spread to his team. I initially thought, "No problem! Simply provide John with constructive feedback and change will follow." After all, John was a great guy. I liked him. However, no matter how hard I tried to help him see his deficiencies and make constructive adjustments, John never changed. He remained oblivious to the obvious.

Next there was Sally. She was undoubtedly the sweetest, hardest working, most dedicated person I had ever encountered. When we hired Sally, I thought she might be the best employee yet. But soon I discovered that Sally was a pathological liar. While she consistently presented her brightest and best side to me, her team often experienced the darkest and worst side of her personality. The "sweet little Sally" that I encountered could chew you up and spit you out for no apparent reason. Whenever I gave Sally feedback, she looked at me as if I was speaking a different language. Despite my most determined efforts, I could not help Sally see the deficiencies that were apparent to me and everyone else. Once again, I failed.

Next came Michael, a great guy that everyone loved. His decision to leave an already successful career to join our company surprised me. Michael's work was always precise. His teammates loved him, but there was one issue. Michael was a perfectionist and struggled with deadlines. Thus, while Michael was striving for excellence, our company's momentum was slowing and the market was passing us by. No matter what I did to assist him in seeing the problem, it remained hidden to him.

After fourteen years as the leader of the company, I felt like a failure. My dream had become a nightmare. Why couldn't I help the people I loved? Why couldn't they see what I saw? It all seemed so obvious and easy to fix. Why did they have to become casualties on my watch?

The Journey to Self-Aware

Then my life changed. At the age of forty-four, following a season of "holy discontent," I began feeling tugged and nudged in the direction of vocational ministry. After a year of prayer for clarity, I left the marketplace and became the executive pastor of a church I had attended for several years.

Managing our staff was one of the primary responsibilities of my new role. Starting out, I remember thinking, "Now I will get a chance to implement all of the great employee growth strategies I developed in the marketplace. Surely if you work in a church, you will be able to recognize your flaws and want to experience transformational change." But I soon realized that marketplace and ministry challenges were very similar when people are involved.

Soon after my new career began, I read Daniel Goleman's international bestseller, *Emotional Intelligence*. Since I was passionate about helping people grow, I was fascinated to learn how a lack of self-awareness prevents growth. Because of my previous failures in assisting employees to recognize their shortcomings and make necessary changes, I was determined to find answers. Goleman's strong emphasis on the necessity of individuals to understand their flaws first, before they can experience change, provided me with a sense of relief and vindication. I even remember thinking, "Perhaps I'm not such a failure after all!"

Thus, I began to focus on my journey into self-awareness. I took all the personality tests I could find. I wanted to know my strengths and weaknesses. I became more willing to uncover the hidden parts of my personality and more open to ways that I could change. Eventually, I began living with the illusion that all my blind spots had been discovered. Sure, I had my flaws, but I was acutely aware of them and certainly open to change. At least, that's what I believed was true.

The Meeting

Then it happened. I was meeting with one of my teams. I had served with this team for several years. I genuinely trusted and loved each member of the group. While sharing with them some strongly held convictions, I began to sense that the meeting wasn't going well. I was confused by the tension in the room. My ideas were well-conceived and my communication was clear, but

I detected an air of resistance and dis-ease among the group. "What's their problem?" I wondered. My judgment was confirmed when the meeting ended and everyone hastily departed. "How could they not see and agree with my ideas?"

Over the years, I had diligently worked to earn their trust and respect. There had been conflicts and disagreements, but we always confronted them head-on. I went home feeling confused, discouraged, and angry.

Over the next week, I had very little engagement with the group. I began to feel shunned and, as each day passed, I became more frustrated. I had given so much to this team!

Finally, one team member informed me that the group wanted to meet regarding their concerns about our interactions in the previous meeting. I began replaying the events in my head. "How could they be concerned? If anyone is concerned, it should be me!"

A few days before the meeting, the Spirit of God began unsettling me. I started fasting the day before the meeting, wanting to make sure my heart was beating in sync with God's.

Once we gathered, our first order of business was to establish our intentions and how to pursue them. Each person would state their concerns, with a shared hope for reconciliation and restoration. The first person said that I had not been myself during the past six months and that several of my remarks and reactions during our last meeting validated his uneasiness. I thanked him for voicing his concerns and apologized for any actions of mine that disturbed or offended him.

The second person recalled a brash and insensitive comment I made at the end of our previous meeting. Instantly, I remember thinking, "She has that wrong.

There is no way I spoke those words! I would never say such a thing!" Wanting to avoid appearing defensive, I remained quiet until she concluded her remarks. I thanked her for sharing her observations, then added, "I believe you misunderstood. I never said what you think you heard." Instantaneously, the entire group responded in unison, "YES YOU DID!"

I was stunned, utterly astonished! How could I possibly not remember speaking words that, clearly, they had heard me say? These beloved and trusted friends offered ample proof that I had a blind spot of epic proportions. To this day, I can't recall saying the words they heard. Had the Evil One hidden this toxic poison so effectively that I truly could not see it? Had it taken root and grown in some dark, hidden corner of my being in such a way that it was manifested in my words and actions without me knowing? Certainly not me—the most self-aware and open person I knew!

We ended our meeting in a far different place than where it began. No one was in a hurry to leave. Instead, we remained together, laughing, praying, and loving each other. I am incredibly grateful to have been surrounded by people who loved me enough to expose a dangerous blind spot in my life. St. Augustine said, "A friend is someone who knows everything about you and still accepts you." Isn't this the dream we all share? Don't we long to have people we trust, who will call attention to our blind spots, while continuing to accept and love us?

Freedom

I woke up the following morning raring to go. I felt more energized and restored than I'd been in a long time. The change was so noticeable that I wondered about the cause. I sat on the edge of the bed and began to replay the events of the previous day. Then I realized that I was experiencing the effects of freedom. For the first time in months, a huge burden had been lifted, like a cancerous tumor successfully removed from my body. So many times, we don't recognize the impact of our blind spots until they are exposed.

I quickly sent a note to the group expressing my gratitude. A newfound longing for others to see their blind spots and experience the same freedom began to stir in me. I wanted others to feel the same release. After all, blind spots are hard to see so they require certain mirrors to look deep inside our soul. God's Word, the work of the Holy Spirit, and doing life in community are three great places to start. God's heart breaks when we choose to allow our blind spots to separate us from him.

A few months later, I walked into my friend Fil Anderson's office to share my experience and seek his counsel. Fil is one of the best teachers of spiritual growth I know. For several years he has been my spiritual mentor, challenging me to come closer and to look deeper. A few years ago, I was able to convince Fil to join our staff. He helped us learn to "be" with Jesus while "doing" for Jesus, especially since our "doing" can hide our blind spots if we aren't careful.

Soon after, our conversations turned to a desire to capture our thoughts and experiences in this book. In fact, one reason we chose to write it was to hold each other accountable for our blind spots!

(Fil)

Living (and Nearly Dying) in a World of Blind Spots

As far back as I can remember, I was hooked on approval. I was driven by the desire to establish my worth and make my mark as a spiritual leader. So, when I was offered an opportunity to become a part-time youth pastor while still in college, I took the plunge. I craved the recognition it provided and yet found myself utterly unprepared for the weight of expectations that came with the title. Immediately, my life became a whirlwind of activity that garnered praise and admiration—and eventually resulted in unintended but horrific consequences.

After a few years of huffing and puffing to gain the favor of God and others, what I feared most finally occurred. The threat of being exposed as an impostor—combined with the fatigue I'd been hiding—ushered me into a state of utter exhaustion and depression. No longer able to hold up the mask, I experienced a physical and emotional breakdown and admitted myself into the psychiatric unit of a local hospital.

For two weeks, I lived behind locked doors with other distraught individuals. My experience might sound like a nightmare to you, but to me, it was the safest, most loving place I'd ever been. There, I was free from the need to care for or impress anyone. Instead, I was surrounded by people who wanted to care for *me*, urging me to rest and assuring me that feeling broken was neither wrong nor a sign of weakness. They affirmed my value at a point when I was incapable of doing anything to prove my worth.

When I left the hospital, I stepped right back into the illusion that the approval my heart desperately yearned for would be discovered in the midst of busyness. How others appraised my work again became the most significant indicator of my worth. My life became a bizarre bundle of paradoxes and blind spots. Despite my contempt for it, I craved the constant activity. Busyness had a narcotic effect, soothing the unbearable pain of alienation, loneliness, anxiety, and fear that plagued me.

When I was busy, I could avoid feeling. While I carefully hid them from view (my own and others'), my repressed feelings were nonetheless releasing a deadly toxin that was attacking the core of my being without my knowing.

A Life-Altering Encounter

Many years later, in the chill of winter, a fifteen-minute conversation changed the trajectory of my life. I was attending a conference and had signed up to meet with the main speaker for something announced as "spiritual direction." Having no concept of what that was, I didn't expect anything significant to happen. Besides, all I wanted was a superficial conversation and a personally signed copy of his new book so that I could brag that he and I were friends.

He began our brief visit by asking about a part of me that I had not considered for quite some time. "Tell me about the condition of your soul," he asked. There was silence.

I was clueless. How could I tell this stranger about a part of me with which I was so unfamiliar? But rather than be found without an answer, I babbled about the most disturbing and familiar aspect of my life: the frenzied, out-of-control pace I couldn't seem to escape. After listening for a while, he made the statement that was the beginning of a change in my life: "Fil, you seem dreadfully close to losing touch with the Jesus you so desperately want others to know."

Never had words pierced my heart as these did. Later, when I was alone, I wondered, "Was this Jesus speaking into my life?" For quite some time I'd had a haunting sensation that certain things in my life were out of control. But there had been no time to analyze the problem, its cause, or what might happen if I didn't rein in the chaos.

12

As I sped down life's highway going in four directions at once, always striving and always busy, I was unaware of some dangerous and potentially deadly blind spots. But after speaking with this holy man and sensing Jesus's nearness, I set out on a spiritual journey toward the recognition of some of the dangerous blind spots and a more authentic life.

Spiritual Blind Spots

I gradually began to recognize the most dangerous blind spot of all: a flawed, destructive concept of God. With unrivaled grace and finesse, Jesus started to lavish on me an ever-increasing awareness of the boundlessness of his love, and my heart was taken captive. He refused to allow me to destroy my life, which I had known was happening.

As far back as I could remember, the primary focus of my attention had been on the needs of others. I had a reputation for acting unselfishly and being helpful, kind, compassionate, supportive, and affirming. These characteristics of my personality came quite naturally. I seemed to have a sixth sense for what others needed and found deep satisfaction in meeting those needs.

For instance, when I was growing up, a family rule was that everyone took their plate to the kitchen sink after a meal. Because I enjoyed such tasks, I often gathered all the dishes and washed them without being asked. I also enjoyed the recognition it garnered from my parents and siblings.

Thinking that my selfless service was what made me lovable and valued to others and to God, I gave without boundaries and dismissed my own needs as irrelevant. I took Jesus's words that "it is better to give than to receive" to a new level. This way of expressing my

God-given gift of love and nurture became for me a blind spot. Deep down, I experienced sadness because I came to believe that I was unlovable as I was. I believed I would be rejected or disliked by God and others if I failed to meet their needs.

So I sought validation by being indispensable. I wanted to be known as the ultimate selfless giver, even to the point of being a rescuer and a martyr. I foolishly imagined that even God must be impressed with how I served sacrificially, without limits. Though service was meaningful and a source of joy, I was prone to over-give. Worse still, if my help was not acknowledged, I felt hurt and slighted. Since I relied on recognition and approval for my unselfish giving, my primary fear was being useless and unable to help.

My besetting sin was pride, but I could not see it. This blind spot manifested itself in two ways. First, I believed that I knew how best to meet another's needs, even better than the one who seemed to need my help. I was proud of my insightfulness, and I wore it as a badge of honor that I awarded myself.

My sinful pride also manifested itself in my denial of my own needs and desires. It felt selfish and wrong to care for myself since this went against my preferred identity as the one who helps God and others. I had a difficult time asking for help and I chronically diverted attention away from my neediness. When people did help, I felt guilty and obligated to repay them rather than merely receiving their help and expressing gratitude.

We Don't See What We Can't See

We are, by definition, unaware of our blind spots. What a revelation it was to realize that I don't always know what I'm doing when I'm doing it! I can't see the damaging effect of my obsessions and compulsions on others or on myself. But I'm not alone. We all have moments when we don't know why we're choosing to live as we do, or we just don't see what we're doing. This is what Jesus was getting at when he asked, ". . . why worry about a speck in your friend's eye when you have a log in your own?" (Matthew 7:3). Our blind spots are the logs in our eyes that we never see. God graciously uses his Word, his people, and his Spirit to show us things about ourselves that we can't or don't want to see.

Our blind spots are like rocks on a dark path. We stumble over them because we can't see them. I, for instance, stumble over my arrogant invasiveness and presumptuous desire to control as I compulsively try to help people.

The problem with our blind spots is not just that they lead us into a life of frustration, disappointment, and feeling overwhelmed with life, others, and ourselves. They are also potent hindrances to our spiritual growth. To the extent that we are blind to what is motivating us, we aren't free to grow. Discovering our blind spots helps us embrace the truth that God has a plan for our lives that's better than ours.

The Puzzle of Ourselves

Discovering our blind spots helps us to find the answer to the question we all must answer: *Who in the world am I?* This is not a narcissistic question (although it can be). It's an essential question.

John Calvin wrote, "Nearly all wisdom we possess . . . consists of two parts: the knowledge of God and of ourselves. . . . The knowledge of ourselves not only arouses us to seek God, but also, as it were, leads us by the hand to find him."[1]

Centuries later, David Benner wrote: "Lack of aware-ness is the ground of our dis-ease and brokenness. . . . Choosing awareness opens us up to finding God in the midst of our present realities. . . . Awareness is the key to so much. This is why it is, in my opinion, the single most important spiritual practice."[2]

These are powerful words from a respected teacher of Christian theology from the sixteenth century and a modern-day teacher of psychology and spirituality. Their wisdom exposes the impact that blind spots can have on our souls and our walk with God.

Our blind spots prevent us from experiencing the unrivaled love of God. If I am hiding behind a blind spot, I am unconsciously keeping God, others, and myself from the unparalleled love God offers. But discovering my blind spots has led me to a level of self-awareness that has drawn me into a richer and fuller awareness of God's unconditional love.

The Truest Truth

Years ago, I had a month-long speaking assignment at a Christian camp in New York. My wife and children were coming with me, but we knew my days would be demanding once we arrived. So we took an entire week to make the trip, allowing for quality time together as a family. I'm glad we did because, upon our arrival, I hit the ground running. Days later, I was sitting in a meet-ing when, out of the corner of my eye, I saw someone pacing back and forth at the end of a long hallway. At first, I gave it no thought. But as the pacing continued, I turned and discovered that it was our three-year-old son, Will. When he passed me, he slowed down and looked in my direction. Wondering what he might be thinking, I waited for the next time he passed and motioned for him to come to me. I pray I never forget the look of sheer joy, relief, and delight on his face. First walking and then running to where I sat waiting, he shouted, "Him wants me! Yes! My daddy wants me!"

What about you? Are your days spent frantically pacing back and forth—wondering, fearing, and dreading how God feels about you? Is God's love for you something you can't see? If so, I have some excellent news. Jesus wants to lead you to the real you, the person you truly are, the person he made you to be. Your view of God, others, and yourself can change, if you'll see yourself as Jesus does—as one who is deeply loved, completely forgiven, and forever free.

Be Encouraged

This is a fantastic fact: People can change. It will not happen if we ignore or deny the dangerous presence of the blind spots in our lives. But with enough raw honesty, willingness to change, and openness to seeing what God and others see in us, change can happen.

Get Engaged

Before moving on, make a list of people you know who have made significant, positive changes in the way they live, looking more like Jesus now than they used to.

CHAPTER 2

What Are Blind Spots?

Unless you learn to face your own shadows, you will continue to see them in others, because the world outside you is only a reflection of the world inside you. — Unknown

(Tim)

Flying Blind

It was a great day for flying. I was still working in my business at the time, and we were in negotiations to purchase a company that would allow us to enter a new market. I had my private pilot license, and the prospective company was four hours away by car, but only a little over an hour by plane. Anytime I could save time and enjoy a day of flying was a good day. I headed to our local airport to get the plane ready. I did my regular pre-flight routine. Everything looked good, so I taxied to the runway.

Earlier that year, I received my instrument rating, which enabled me to file a flight plan to ensure that air traffic control (ATC) could track my progress. They would be my eyes in the sky. I always welcomed the extra support. I also used additional technology for backup in case of an emergency. Although I utilized a GPS to navigate in the plane, I always carried a handheld GPS backup just in case, along with a bag full of batteries. Finally, I had a storm tracking device to alert me to any changes in weather. Bad weather and a single-engine airplane do not mix well.

The flight was rather uneventful. As I lifted off the runway, I immediately called for ATC to open my flight plan: "Greensboro approach, 440 Bravo, Bravo departing Burlington heading to Anderson, SC." Soon ATC responded with the heading and altitude I needed to proceed. Eventually, one ATC tower handed me off to the next as I made my way. I engaged the autopilot, put on some music, and waited for further instructions. At various times ATC would provide traffic advisories. "440 Bravo, Bravo be aware of traffic at seven thousand feet at your one o'clock position." It was always a comforting voice keeping me posted on potential blind spots in the air.

About twenty minutes from Anderson, I noticed something. I suddenly realized that my radio was quiet. I hadn't heard anything from ATC in a while. I clicked the mic and said, "Anderson approach, 440 Bravo, Bravo do you copy?" In a few seconds ATC responded: "440 Bravo, Bravo go ahead." I then informed them of the silence to make sure everything was OK.

At that point, I felt an ache in the pit of my stomach. "440 Bravo, Bravo we don't see you on radar, please ident." I immediately pressed a button that highlights my image on their screen for tracking. Then I heard, "440 Bravo, Bravo it appears that we have lost radar contact. What's your current location?" I gave my best guess, but I had been on autopilot, letting the plane do the work. My details were sketchy. Also, at that point, I was starting to run into a few clouds. Losing radar contact when you can't see and be seen is not good! Finally, ATC informed me that they still couldn't track me, but they would try to keep me abreast of any traffic in the area. I was flying blind and needed to navigate the rest of the way myself. My heart was racing as I struggled to watch for additional traffic.

Soon I arrived at the Anderson airport and landed safely, but the ache in the pit of my stomach didn't go away for a while. The thought of being surprised by another large piece of metal flying at hundreds of miles per hour on a partially cloudy day was unnerving. However, we are often comfortable allowing it to happen every day in our personal lives!

What Are They?

Even though the words "blind spots" are familiar and straightforward, they are often hard to see and understand. Typically, blind spots are associated with our inability to see when we are doing things like changing lanes in a car, losing track of something in our peripheral vision, or even flying blind without the help of ATC.

The clarity of our vision is typically measured by the eye chart at the doctor's office. We assume that twenty-twenty vision is the gold standard; however, having twenty-twenty vision does not necessarily mean that you have perfect vision: twenty-twenty vision only indicates the sharpness or clarity of vision at a specific distance of twenty feet. Other significant vision skills, including peripheral awareness, eye coordination, depth perception, focusing ability, and color vision all contribute to your overall visual ability.

Still, people with twenty-twenty vision tend to think they can see everything in their surroundings. However, no matter how hard you try, you cannot see everything around you. The human eye has a blind spot; a small area on the retina, approximately the size of a pencil eraser, without photoreceptors. We are typically unaware of this blind spot because our brain fills in this blank with the surrounding images, making our visual field appear seamless, creating an optical illusion. But there are other blind spots that are not related to our eyesight. These blind spots take up residence in our mind and soul and directly affect our spiritual, personal, and professional growth. We often refer to these blind spots as cognitive. A person may have a blind spot in an area or subject where he is uninformed or prejudiced, or where he has been hurt or deceived, causing gaps in perception that blind them from seeing the truth about themselves and others. These blind spots keep our minds from seeing reality. They blind us to additional possibilities that are before us. They can immobilize and cripple us, creating guilt and shame, anger and bitterness, worry and regret, fear and anxiety.

These blind spots can leave their mark in all areas of our lives. When a blind spot affects us spiritually, we start to live on autopilot as we allow other things to distract us from our time with God. Spiritual practices that once seemed rich and powerful are now simply items to check off a list. We lose our personal connection with God because we allow other things to take his place.

Personally, blind spots can cause relationships between good friends to become fractured and broken. Marriages crumble because one spouse is unwilling to see what the other sees. Parents wake up one morning to find their precious teenager in trouble. At first they are

21

shocked, but then they realize that they have been blindly looking the other way for months.

Blind spots permeate our workplaces. We are frustrated with management's inability to see the obstacles that prevent future growth. Or perhaps we do not see the flaws in our performance that result in a poor review or even a termination.

Lots of people live needlessly in misery and defeat, paralyzed by their own mistakes. Often they stumble and fumble their way through life, hindering the work of God in their lives. But here's the good news: It doesn't have to be this way! No matter how foolish or misguided, every person can discover a life in which they can face their blind spots. Transformational change can occur!

Blinded by the Light

Many times blind spots disguise themselves as worthy and righteous causes while they lead us down a path of disruption. Perhaps the most famous example in Scripture involved a man named Saul of Tarsus. Not only did Saul's life change, but his name changed as well. He came to be known as the apostle Paul and he wrote most of the New Testament epistles we study today.

Saul began life as a devout Jew. He was passionate about his faith and determined to remove any obstacle or opposition to it. He later recalls:

> "I am a Jew, born in Tarsus, a city in Cilicia, and I was brought up and educated here in Jerusalem under Gamaliel. As his student, I was carefully trained in our Jewish laws and customs. I became very zealous to honor God in everything I did, just like all of you today." (Acts 22:3)

Paul was so zealous that he was confident that he was doing the right thing, serving God devoutly by defending his faith. But a spiritual blind spot distorted his vision and could have destroyed his life. We first meet Paul (then Saul) at the end of Acts 7, when Stephen, a deacon in the Christian church in Jerusalem, became its first martyr when he was stoned to death. Saul was present as an innocent or maybe not-so-innocent bystander.

> Then they put their hands over their ears and began shouting. They rushed at him [Stephen] and dragged him out of the city and began to stone him. His accusers took off their coats and laid them at the feet of a young man named Saul. (Acts 7:57–58)

Immediately persecution of the Christ followers ensued, causing them to flee from Jerusalem to seek refuge in other cities and countries. Some traveled as far away as 150 miles north to Damascus in Syria. Damascus was a key commercial city with important trade routes linking it to cities throughout the Roman world. Saul was determined to track these Christ followers down and eliminate this new faith group before it spread like a dangerous disease.

> Meanwhile, Saul was uttering threats with every breath and was eager to kill the Lord's followers. So he went to the high priest. He requested letters addressed to the synagogues in Damascus, asking for their cooperation in the arrest of any followers of the Way he found there. He wanted to bring them—both men and women—back to Jerusalem in chains. (Acts 9:1–2)

Saul's spiritual blindness convinced him that he was doing the right thing. He didn't realize that his persecution of Christians meant that he was actually persecuting the Son sent by God. Saul had become an enemy to the very God he had pledged to protect. It would take something radical to change his mind and God had just the thing: a flash of light.

> As he [Saul] was approaching Damascus on this mission, a light from heaven suddenly shone down around him. He fell to the ground and heard a voice saying to him, "Saul! Saul! Why are you persecuting me?" (Acts 9:3–4)

As Saul was blinded by the heavenly light, his next question was obvious.

> "Who are you, lord?" Saul asked.
> And Jesus replied: "I am Jesus, the one you are persecuting! Now get up and go into the city, and you will be told what you must do." (Acts 9:5–6)

Imagine what was going through Saul's mind at this point. He thought he'd been pursuing a group of heretics, but according to the voice, Paul was attacking God himself, the one he thought he was defending.

Many times our blindness causes us to attack the wrong person for what we believe are the right reasons. Often our pride does not allow us to see this misfortune. But in Saul's case, his spiritual blindness and pride were eliminated when he lost his physical sight, in an act of God's grace.

The men with Saul stood speechless, for they heard the sound of someone's voice but saw no one! Saul picked himself up off the ground, but when he opened his eyes, he was blind. So his companions led him by the hand to Damascus. He remained there blind for three days and did not eat or drink. (Acts 9:7–9)

Ironically Saul's physical blindness led to the removal of his spiritual blindness. His encounter with Jesus led him to join the ranks of those he had felt called to persecute. Without this encounter, Paul could have spent the remainder of his life blindly fighting against the God he thought he was serving. Sometimes it takes a wake-up call to realign our efforts with God's plan for our lives. Otherwise we function outside the will of God. Paul's wake-up call launched him on a journey to expose the spiritual blind spots of others and introduce them to Jesus.

Aha Moments

Paul's encounter at Damascus certainly qualifies as an "aha moment." I've often thought that for change to happen, an awakening has to occur. Some are more radical than others. Usually, we don't ease into awareness; it often makes a dramatic entrance. Merriam-Webster defines an "aha moment" as "a moment of sudden realization, inspiration, insight, recognition, or comprehension." That certainly was Paul's experience!

Aha moments can knock us off our feet like an unexpected medical diagnosis. Perhaps we thought we could escape the pains of exercise and eating our veggies until the doctor informs us that we are one step away from a heart attack. Or, maybe even more traumatic, we ignore the doctor and our aha moment is the actual heart attack that we are fortunate enough to survive. There's the aha moment when a spouse reveals their dissatisfaction in a marriage. Over and over, they've tried to get your attention. Now, as a last resort, the only thing left to do is leave. Are you really surprised or did you need an aha moment to wake you up?

What about the aha moment when your manager walks into your office to inform you that you are no longer needed? He'd tried to emphasize your poor performance and negative team interactions. You knew that you could be difficult at times, but you'd convinced yourself that it was just the way you were and others needed to get over it. Your aha moment comes to reveal your blind spot when your boss decides to let some other company wrestle with your dysfunction.

Financial aha moments can occur when you look over the credit card bill at the end of the month. You had no idea you were spending at the speed of light! How did it all add up to this amount? I remember my first financial aha moment as a teenager. We had joined a local country club so I could practice tennis with some of my high school teammates. After a long workout one day my friend said, "Let's go to the snack bar." I informed him that I didn't have any money. He said, "No problem, all you have to do is charge it." Wow, that was amazing and easy! I soon became a fan of this new system, until my dad provided an aha moment when he got the bill.

You can discover the aha moment or the aha moment can discover you. The first is enlightening and manageable, followed by growth. The second still provides an opportunity for growth but is more painful.

During my training to fly a single-engine airplane, I had an opportunity to go to Wichita, Kansas, for training.

Lots of flight training happens there. I guess all the open fields of Kansas help to eliminate blind spots! The training consisted of time in the classroom, the flight simulator, and actual time in the airplane. Most of my training in the simulator prepared me for handling emergencies. Repeatedly the flight instructor put me through the paces of situational awareness, forcing me to think in the air. Quick decisions are a necessity, and you never want to be caught without a plan. Flying is not a time for surprises that leave you wondering what to do next.

During one particular session, the instructor looked at me and said, "OK, you are flying at night and you just lost electrical power to all your navigational devices. What are you going to do?" Being a fan of backups upon backups while flying, I said, "I will pull out my handheld GPS and continue to navigate." The instructor, with a smirk on his face, decided to play along. "What if the batteries in the handheld GPS are dead?" I replied, "I will pull out my ziplock bag with all my extra batteries." The instructor decided to put an end to this charade. "And what if all the extra batteries in your little ziplock bag are dead?" At that point, I said, "I guess the good Lord wants me to die!" Aha moments are better managed when *you* find *them* as opposed to having them find you!

Finding the Aha Moments

The problem with proactively finding the aha moments is that most people don't know where to begin to look. We either line up on one end of the spectrum or the other. First, because of our pride and ego, we become convinced that our abilities are more significant than they are. This personality trait is called the Dunning–Kruger effect,[1] which creates a blind spot of deception, where the less skilled you are at something, the less likely you are to realize how unskilled you are. Bad drivers are a great example. My kids always complain about my driving. I, on the other hand, think I'm a great driver! In reality, I'm probably a prime candidate for Dunning-Kruger.

At the other end of the spectrum, we might underestimate our abilities even when we improve in specific areas of our lives. This personality trait is called the impostor syndrome,[2] which is an internalized fear of being exposed as a fraud. Our insecurity convinces us that we don't deserve the success we have achieved, so we allow our impostor blind spot to take control. From a biblical perspective, this could reflect a fear and unbelief regarding the promises of God that apply to us.

Several years ago, I was given the opportunity to speak to a large group. Immediately I was intimidated by the idea; I never considered myself a public speaker. But one talk led to another and another, and to date I have given hundreds of talks to groups of all sizes. It has become a passion of mine and I love the opportunity to communicate, though early on I was a victim of the impostor syndrome. Often I was afraid my communication gift from God was a fraud. I couldn't accept that it was something I should actually pursue. It wasn't until several others and the Holy Spirit affirmed the gift that my impostor blind spot was exposed, and I began to follow God's plans for my life.

Struggles like these internal battles can make it difficult to proactively find our aha moments. But there is hope. A willingness to ask questions is the first step. Here are a few that might help you begin the journey.

- Is there a pattern or theme in your life that appears again and again?

- Do you have a habit that is hurtful or harmful to your joy and well-being?
- Do you regularly feel anxious, overwhelmed, insecure, or frustrated?
- Do you feel tension in a relationship and you can't put your finger on the issue?
- Is there an area in your life that you are struggling to manage?
- Do you have any behaviors or experiences that happen repetitively in your career?
- How would you rate your productivity?
- Do you struggle to focus on the task at hand?
- What things do you find difficult to say to others?
- Are you continually running late for appointments?
- Do you value being right over being effective?
- Do you struggle and say "yes" to people when you should say "no"?
- Do you say "yes" too often?
- Are you impatient when things don't happen as quickly as you want?
- Do you struggle to stand up for yourself in conflict?
- Do you find yourself settling for less than you want in life because you think you are not worth it?

If you feel really brave, answer each of these questions on a scale of one to five, one meaning "Never" and five meaning "Holy cow, yes, that's me!" Ask a few trusted friends and family members to rate you as well. The gaps will expose your blind spots!

"Unless you learn to face your own shadows, you will continue to see them in others, because the world outside you is only a reflection of the world inside you" (Author unknown).

Be Encouraged

Once you accept that you don't always see things as they are and you recognize the considerable threat that blind spots pose to yourself and others, the real transformative work begins. Three life-altering things can occur:

- Humility begins to develop.
- We become open and submissive to the Holy Spirit's direction in our lives.
- We stop judging ourselves and other people.

Jesus said in John 8:32: "And you will know the truth, and the truth will set you free" (ESV). The truth will allow you to stop flying blind through life's journey.

Get Engaged

Take a minute to answer the questions listed above. Rank your answers to each question from one to five; one indicating never and five indicating a resounding yes to the question. Then ask two other people (perhaps a family member and a close friend or coworker) to answer the same questions on your behalf. Highlight any answers that vary more than one point from your answers. Spend time in prayer, asking God how he wants you to address these potential blind spots.

CHAPTER 3

Why Are They Blind?

The only thing worse than being blind is having sight but no vision. — Helen Keller

(Tim)

The Text Poll

It was a beautiful sunny day in early February, and my son Fletcher and I were headed to central Florida for a college visit. When we left North Carolina, the temperatures were close to freezing, but we were headed for warmer weather.

Fletcher was driving, and after chatting for a bit, we settled into our spaces. He was listening to music on the radio, and I was answering a few e-mails and text messages. At that point I was reminded of a recent staff assignment and took the opportunity to send a short survey to my family by text.

Over the years my family has served as a stellar focus group. I can always count on them for input, no matter how brutally honest it might be. Also, since our family is relatively large, the sample rate is excellent. Fletcher has three sisters, two older and one younger. At the time they ranged in ages from fourteen to twenty-four and they were not afraid to share their opinions! My wife Stacy and I complete the group of six, though this time my vote didn't count.

The staff assignment at church was from a few weeks earlier, when our entire team at St. Mark's Church (SMC) gathered for our first monthly meeting of the new year. The meeting was significant because it would set the tone for the entire year. I was responsible for leading the session as executive pastor. Our team had just completed a nine-week small group discussion on our staff values, which had prepared us for this day.

The previous year our leadership team had decided to identify our values. We wrestled with several universal marketplace values like integrity, respect, excellence, responsibility, teamwork, and many more. For some reason, they all seemed stale to me. I had read them over and over in all the bestselling books on leadership, so perhaps I had become numb to their meaning.

That's when it hit me. I remembered Paul's teaching about the fruit of the Spirit in Galatians 5.

> But the Holy Spirit produces this kind of fruit in our lives: love, joy, peace, patience, kindness, goodness, faithfulness, gentleness, and self-control. (Galatians 5:22–23)

Here were the values that represented who we wanted to be, not only as Christ followers but as teammates at SMC. Our team spent nine weeks looking deeply into each fruit and its significance.

So, on the first meeting of the new year, I suggested that we each pick one fruit to focus on for the year.

I understand that Paul never intended for us to cherry-pick these fruits; the nine are considered one. But how do you eat an elephant? One bite at a time! One of the directives of our team was to seek advice. I instructed everyone to ask their family and close friends which fruit they thought should be their focus for the year. Obviously, it would be a fruit that needed a little nourishment to grow. This was the question I wanted to ask my family.

I composed the question, explained the context and asked which fruit my family thought needed the extra attention. Off it went into cyberspace and I waited. In just a few minutes, my phone dinged and I quickly looked, anxious to see the response. It was from one of my daughters, and it simply said "patience." At first glance it stung a little, but I thought, "Hang in there, there's still time for things to turn around." A few minutes later another ding came in, and it also said, "patience." Shortly after that, another vote for patience arrived. Three down, two to go. (Remember, I didn't get a vote this time.) The fourth vote rang loud and clear and was consistent with the others. Finally, I looked at Fletcher and said, "What's your vote?" He hadn't seen the replies because he was driving, but he quickly said "patience." Well, at least I had clarity!

To be honest, I wasn't surprised. If I had done my homework before the poll and looked intently at all nine fruits, patience would have risen to the top. But why wasn't I one hundred percent sure? Why did I need to take the poll? Why did their responses sting a little? I had allowed a blind spot of denial to develop around my lack of patience.

Blind Spots of Denial

I think we all would agree that everyone has a blind spot or two in their lives. But why is that? Why can't we see the things that others see in us? Why do we need to send a text poll to our family and friends to uncover our blind spots?

Sometimes these are things that are genuinely hidden from our view. We have no idea they are lurking in the shadows of our soul. A friend compared it to that certain spot in a rearview mirror where an eighteen-wheeler truck can suddenly disappear. He drove a school bus in his younger days, and in his training, he was alerted to the fact that, if a truck was in that perfect position, he would not see it in the school bus mirror. I guess some blind spots find the ideal location to hide no matter how large they are!

But at other times, our willful denial of certain facts in our lives is what makes them blind spots. We don't want to see them, and after a while, we don't. An issue conveniently and consistently denied over time doesn't disappear, but our hearts and souls become numb to its existence. We subconsciously learn how to ensure that it doesn't create too much chaos in our lives. It may emerge from time to time, but quickly we stuff it back into a corner of our soul. The more we follow this routine, the more it becomes our way of life.

For example, a functioning alcoholic learns how to deny his disease by managing his addiction during the day so that others can't see it. In the evenings it may rear its ugly head, but for just a few eyes to see.

A husband and father who is addicted to pornography denies the severity of his viewing habits. He tells himself, "What harm could it do in the privacy of my home?" The first time he indulges in this sinful behavior, he feels really bad. The next time he feels a little less bad. Each time he feels less and less guilt until he convinces himself that as long as he keeps it hidden, there is little harm done. He numbs his conscience until his sin is out of sight and mind. Until it begins to affect his relationship with others, it may never be detected even though it is slowly destroying his life.

A controlling wife might tell herself that she is the one in the family who has to get things done. She tells herself that she is the one who has to juggle the kids, her job, and her marriage. She feels underappreciated and can't understand why the family isn't more grateful for all she does. She doesn't allow herself to see that she dominates things so much that everyone else feels suffocated. She doesn't trust anyone else to do things "the right way" and in her eyes, everyone else's value begins to diminish. But she is so determined to be right and to do things her way, she cannot see the damage she is doing to the family she professes to love. However, because of her denial she keeps the blind spot on a tight leash so that it doesn't destroy her life.

Living in denial can bring a false sense of security. The problem that's been hidden away may surface from time to time, but refusing to see what's there is a way to put off the issue for another day, hoping that it will eventually resolve itself. One of the most important components of Alcoholics Anonymous is the regular small group meetings. I have a friend who has been sober for twenty years but he still attends meetings. Why? He doesn't want to live in denial about his addiction, so that his problem finds another hiding place. He wants to be in a place where friends who know him well can point out his blind spots.

Are You Aware?

A friend of mine has a company that works with colleges and universities. One of the services they provide is an atmospheric assessment. They arrive on campus early in the morning and spend all day taking pictures of things that look out of place. Then they compile a presentation for the president the next day. After the report, the response is always the same. As the president watches the images scroll across the screen, he is amazed at how he and his staff missed these glaring issues. Although they walk past them daily, they had become invisible. They simply didn't see the paint that needed to be refreshed, the doors that needed repair, and the trash that had overflowed out of the dumpster. Their minds were focused on other priorities and soon these issues vanished from their minds.

We may be blind to an issue in our lives because we truly can't see it. Or we may be blind because we often become so obsessed with our agendas that we miss the priorities of others. Even though our physical eyesight may be twenty-twenty, our awareness eyesight can be legally blind. Soon we become oblivious to our surroundings as we live in our own little worlds.

Simon, Do You See This Woman?

By contrast, Jesus was someone with perfect vision. He had no blind spots of any kind, and he regularly exposed the blindness of those who thought they had tremendous insight. In Luke 7 Jesus asks Simon the Pharisee a question. It's simple yet profound. Jesus asks Simon, "Do you see this woman?" (Luke 7:44 NIV).

Simon had invited Jesus to his house for dinner. Simon and the rest of the Pharisees couldn't figure Jesus out. Nobody had ever said the things Jesus was saying. His teaching was radically different from anything they had experienced before. Also, no one had done the things Jesus was doing. Mobs of people were following him daily to glean from his teaching and perhaps witness a miracle.

Jesus is reclining at Simon's table, along with the others Simon had invited. Perhaps some of Simon's colleagues were there, as Simon was probably looking for additional insight to evaluate Jesus. Or maybe he was trying to gather dirt to discredit him.

Then someone else walks in. It's a woman, and not just any woman; it's that "sinful" woman. Somehow she discovered that Jesus was having dinner at Simon's home. She was neither invited nor welcome, but she was determined to deliver a gift to Jesus. She walks in and stands behind him. She is overcome with emotion and begins to cry. Her tears hit his feet. She notices, kneels in front of him, and wipes his dirty, dusty feet with her hair. She then pours the perfume she brought on Jesus's feet.

As Simon watches, he is disgusted both with the woman and Jesus. He says to himself, "If this man were a prophet, he would know who is touching him and what kind of woman she is—that she is a sinner" (Luke 7:39 NIV).

Jesus senses Simon's disgust and begins to tell a story about forgiveness. Jesus compared the fate of two debtors. One owed a lot and the other a little. Both debts were cancelled by the lender. Jesus asks Simon which debtor would be most grateful for the forgiveness. Simon provides the obvious answer, the one with the largest debt. Then Jesus asks Simon a question that would shift the narrative and shatter the perspectives in the room. Jesus said, "Do you see this woman?" (Luke 7:44 NIV).

What did Jesus mean? Was Jesus teaching Simon a lesson about looking versus really seeing? Simon saw only the sinner, the woman she had been. He did not see the change that had come because she had encountered Jesus. He did not see the love, gratitude, humility, and compassion that flowed out of her awareness that her debt of sin had been forgiven. Jesus was challenging Simon to stop looking at who the woman had been and start seeing who she had become.

Did you know there is a difference between looking and seeing? Looking takes but a second, but seeing requires us to look more deeply to understand. Sometimes that seeing challenges the ways a person assumes the world operates. Jesus is asking Simon to stop looking and start seeing.

Not only did Simon not truly see the woman, he did not truly see himself, as Jesus goes on to show him. He says, "'I came into your house. You did not give me any water for my feet, but she wet my feet with her tears and wiped them with her hair. You did not give me a kiss, but this woman, from the time I entered, has not stopped kissing my feet. You did not put oil on my head, but she has poured perfume on my feet. Therefore, I tell you, her many sins have been forgiven—for she loved much. But he who has been forgiven little loves little.' Then Jesus said to her, 'Your sins are forgiven'" (Luke 7:44–48 NIV).

Simon did not see because he had a blind spot, not physically, but in his heart. He couldn't comprehend why Jesus would spend time with someone like this woman. She did not conform to all the things Simon believed constituted spiritual worth, value, or righteousness. And his hospitality—or lack of it—to Jesus revealed that Jesus did not meet his standards either.

Jesus is asking Simon to dig deeper to see what lies beneath the way he looked at the woman and treated Jesus. Could it be a blind spot of self-righteousness? Simon was part of a group that kept score by the number of religious rules they followed each day. Simon knew that his team could outscore his opponents any day of the week. This woman's sins were obvious. She was no match for Simon—that is, if God cared about keeping score. But when Jesus told the woman that her sins were forgiven, he wanted Simon to see that he had missed the point, the whole reason that Jesus came. He was saying, "Dig deep, Simon, because something deep inside you is causing your inability to see."

Peeling Back the Layers

Our blind spots can be hard to see because they hide behind other issues, hoping to distract us from the real, hidden root of the problem. To find the real blind spot, we have to search our hearts and start peeling back the layers.

For example, bitterness is often something that is hard to see in ourselves. Jealousy might be easier to acknowledge, but we certainly don't want to admit that we are bitter. And it's true that bitterness rarely exists alone. It is often accompanied by jealousy, contempt, or gossip that can keep us from seeing the bitterness that runs deeper. Hebrews 12 talks about the root of bitterness.

> Watch out that no poisonous root of bitterness grows up to trouble you, corrupting many. (Hebrews 12:15)

Roots are usually not seen, but they can cause significant damage to pipes, sidewalks, and roads if they grow out of control. A hidden, diseased root can destroy things that grow above the ground, like the visible part of a tree. A poisonous root of bitterness hidden in the corner of our soul can slowly destroy our lives. If we focus on its more surface manifestations like jealousy, contempt, or gossip, our lives may continue to deteriorate because we haven't uncovered the root of the problem.

Anger is another sin that rarely exists alone. I remember one evening, my wife Stacy was late getting home. I tried to call her, but her phone was off because of the meeting she had been attending. As time passed, I started to worry. Minute by minute I grew more anxious. I allowed my imagination to take over, convincing me that something terrible had happened. Then my phone rang. It was Stacy, letting me know that she had stopped by the grocery store to pick up a few things and ran into one of our friends. They had been chatting for a while and lost track of time. Anger influenced my first response. However, when she arrived, I apologized and explained that my anger was actually hiding my fear. I was fearful that something tragic had happened, but a layer of anger disguised it. Focusing on my anger would not uncover my blind spot of fear. Anger was the front man while fear hid in the shadows of my soul. I needed to face both.

Let's go back to my blindness about my impatience. While writing this chapter, I began to wonder if my impatience was a layer covering still another blind spot. After deep soul searching, I began to realize that there are times when I allow my passion to cloud my vision. I can convince myself that my lack of patience is because I am striving for the greater good. If someone stands in my way and they don't line up with my beliefs and values, my impatience feels justified. But when I look deeper, I see that my impatience is often covering up a sense of entitlement that is even harder for me to see. If I am brutally honest, I know that there are times I am impatient because I feel entitled to feel that way. I have valued myself over someone else, and it is revealed in my impatience. I can do everything I can to nurture my fruit of patience, but it will never grow if I don't deal with the sin that my impatience is covering up. If I don't deal with my sense of entitlement along with my impatience, both issues will spill over into other areas of my life. I need to bring both to Jesus, for his forgiveness and his power to change me. I need to wrestle with the same questions the apostle Paul did, recognizing that these are not just issues of the mind, but of the heart.

I don't really understand myself, for I want to do what is right, but I don't do it. Instead, I do what I hate. (Romans 7:15)

Singer-songwriter Travis Meadows writes about these dangerous layers in his song "Sideways." Unaddressed, they can destroy a life. Meadows tells about a time he spoke at a treatment center after a period of addiction of his own. He listened to a young girl bitterly share that drugs had robbed her of any emotion. The counselor, noticing her anger, said, "If all you have is a hammer, then you will treat the whole world like a nail. You've got more emotions than just anger, and it's OK to use them, because if you push it down, it comes out sideways." Meadows wrote these words shortly after that encounter.

If I could buy myself a conscience that wasn't broken,
Mend every fence I drove my hard head through,
Re-lock all the doors I wish I never opened,
Unlearn the things I wish I never knew,
And it came out through the bottle,

41

It came out through my fists,
It came out way too early,
I wish it never did.

Push it down, it comes out sideways.
Push it down, it comes out sideways.
Bitter roads turn into highways,
Push it down, it comes out sideways.[1]

Be Encouraged

Although you may be anxious to identify and remove your blind spots, understanding why we can't see them is the first step. Whether they are completely hidden, denied and conveniently ignored, or hidden behind a few layers, you can identify and ultimately expose them. Starting with why is the first step. Unless we understand "why," we can't get to the root of the problem. And we can't bring that root to God.

Although the process of asking why might be scary, it is the first step to keep your blind spots from controlling your life. A friend of mine always says, "Reality is your friend." Asking why is the first step to seeing what is reality in your life. Helen Keller once said, "The only thing worse than being blind is having sight but no vision." The fact that you are reading this book is encouraging. You are taking a step to uncover the things in your life that might be preventing you from being all that God wants you to be.

Get Engaged

Take a minute to reflect on a few blind spots that may be hiding in your soul. Perhaps you can ask some close friends or family to pick the one fruit of the Spirit that needs the most attention in your life. Spend time in prayer asking God to unveil these hidden layers. Ask him to reveal why you are so comfortable with denial, perhaps why you have stopped feeling the negative impact these issues—these blind spots—are having on your life. And ask him to help you stop hiding from him, but instead to rely on his forgiveness and love to renew your heart and your life.

CHAPTER 4

Is This a New Problem?

The longest journey is the journey inwards.

— Dag Hammarskjold

(Tim)
When I talk about blind spots with people, someone will often ask, "Is this a new problem or has it been around for a while?" Let's take a walk through history to find out.

Ships that Can't See

In the early 1900s the *Titanic* was the largest, most luxurious ocean liner in the world. It created quite a buzz and was considered unsinkable. On April 10, 1912, 2,223 people boarded the *Titanic* for her maiden voyage, with 1,324 passengers and 908 crew. The vessel left Southhampton, England, and headed to New York City. It could carry thirty-two lifeboats that could hold approximately 2,200 people, but only twenty lifeboats were on the maiden voyage. Reports indicate that there was concern that the decks were too cluttered, so the extra lifeboats were left behind.[1] Perhaps that was the first of many blind spots involved in one of the most famous disasters in history, where 1,503 of the 2,223 on board died. There are many opinions as to what went wrong. The bottom line: the ship hit ice. The question that lingers to this day is why they didn't *see* the iceberg. One possibility emerges from the testimony of Fred Fleet, who survived the tragedy. Fleet was the lookout, whose job was to watch for ice. Why didn't he see the iceberg that caused the collision? When he testified before a Senate inquiry, Fleet stated that he wasn't using binoculars. Many believe the binoculars were on the ship but were locked in a cabinet. The key didn't make the voyage. It was in the pocket of the ship's second officer, David Blair, who was replaced at the last minute by Charles Lightoller, who had more experience with larger ships. Some believe that the crew realized that the key was missing after the voyage began but determined it wasn't significant. Their eyes would be sufficient! The binoculars may or may not have prevented the tragedy, but they could have helped the crew avoid a blind spot about an iceberg that led to the sinking of the ship.

Hidden Horses

In the twelfth century BC, the walls of Troy were impenetrable. Even the massive Greek army could not break through. So they tried a different strategy, one for which the Trojans had a blind spot!

The Greeks pretended to retreat and sail to the nearby island of Tenedos. As an apparent peace offering to the gods, they left behind a giant wooden horse, along with Sinon, a Greek soldier who was then captured by the Trojan army. Sinon convinced the Trojans that the horse was an offering to the goddess Athena, and it would be displeasing to the gods to leave the offering outside the gates.

But Cassandra, the daughter of Priam (the king of Troy), tried to warn the people of potential deception. She knew something was up. She suspected a hidden agenda that everyone else was missing. However, the people ignored Cassandra, and the horse was brought in through the gates. The next night while Troy slept, Greek warriors quietly emerged from the horse. They opened the gates of Troy and allowed the hidden Greek army to enter. Quickly the impenetrable city of Troy was under siege and soon fell, all because someone failed to inspect the horse!

Winning at All Costs

Lance Edward Gunderson was born on September 18, 1971. He would become one of the most famous cyclists in history. His more familiar name is Lance Armstrong. He won seven Tour de France titles, considered the pinnacle of cycling success. He is also a cancer survivor and a huge advocate for cancer research. Livestrong, the organization he founded, has raised millions for cancer research and support.

Armstrong was known as a ruthless competitor on and off the bike. If you ended up on the wrong side of Lance, your career could be in jeopardy. He routinely fought rumors that he used performance-enhancing drugs. When accusations came, he vehemently denied every claim. He retired from racing in 2005 but in January 2009, he decided to make a comeback. Later that year, Armstrong finished third in the Tour de France. He retired a second time in 2011.

In 2012, the United States Anti-Doping Agency concluded that Armstrong had used performance-enhancing drugs over the course of his career. Armstrong was named the ringleader of the most sophisticated doping program the sport had ever seen. After a long battle, Armstrong chose not to continue the fight. Stripped from his record were his achievements from August 1988 forward, including his seven Tour De France titles. He received a lifetime ban from all sports that follow the World Anti-Doping Code, which ended his competitive career.

In January 2013, Armstrong acknowledged his misdeeds in an interview with Oprah Winfrey, admitting that he had indeed taken PEDs throughout his career. His admission cost him millions of dollars in sponsorships and endorsements. His hidden offenses tarnished his legacy and many relationships along the way.

Deceptive Blind Spots

In Genesis 3, we meet the mastermind behind all blind spots. When we look at the creation story and Adam and Eve's fall into sin, we may be tempted to ask, How could Adam and Eve make such a terrible mistake? God's instructions to them were clear. They were living in a beautiful garden. God met all their needs. But a new character slithers into the story and brings with him a fatal blind spot.

His plan begins with a question. The first step in the serpent's strategy was to create doubt. Many times our blindness to the truth starts when small, subtle questions are raised that distract us from the truth.

The serpent was the shrewdest of all the wild animals the Lord God had made. One day he asked the woman, "Did God really say you must not eat the fruit from any of the trees in the garden?" (Genesis 3:1)

The woman is strong at first. She corrects the sly serpent: God didn't say they couldn't eat from "any" tree; they simply could not eat from a specific tree in the middle of the garden. But the serpent's question had already put her at a greater distance from the truth, because she adds to God's commandment, saying that they had been commanded not to touch it, which God had not said.

> "Of course we may eat fruit from the trees in the garden," the woman replied. "It's only the fruit from the tree in the middle of the garden that we are not allowed to eat. God said, 'You must not eat it or even touch it; if you do, you will die.'" (Genesis 3:2–3)

Next, the serpent continues to twist the narrative just a little further. As Eve's hold on the truth is altered, her blind spot grows. At the beginning, with the serpent's first question, his lies are imperceptible, but the longer his lies go unchallenged, the more the gap widens between the serpent's story and God's truth, and the more easily Eve is blinded.

> "You won't die!" the serpent replied to the woman. "God knows that your eyes will be opened as soon as you eat it, and you will be like God, knowing both good and evil." (Genesis 3:4–5)

With this open challenge to God, the serpent moves the spotlight from what the man and woman have to what they are supposedly missing. What would life be like if their eyes were open? Wouldn't it be amazing to know good and evil?

When you put it that way, Eve seems to be thinking, perhaps the serpent makes a lot of sense. Why would God want to keep something good from us? How bad can it be? Perhaps we could even be more helpful to God if we expand our knowledge. And in one sense, what the serpent said was true. God did know that if they ate from the tree in the middle of the garden, their eyes would open to new information. They would recognize good and evil. But God also knew that Adam and Eve would be forever changed by that knowledge. It would be an experiential knowledge that would cause sin to become part of their very nature. But that was something the serpent did not want Adam and Eve to see.

Blinded by their desire for independence and autonomy, Adam and Eve decide to walk down this path. What harm could it do? They soon found out. Scripture says their eyes opened "at that moment" and immediately they felt shame in their nakedness. No enlightenment accompanied their newfound knowledge. Instead they covered their shame with fig leaves and for the first time, hid from God in the darkness. Their desire to be like God, independently, had estranged them—and their descendants—from him. The rest of the Bible tells how God fulfilled his promise in Genesis 3:15 to rescue humanity from sin and restore them to a relationship with him that Adam and Eve had lost.

Blind Spots Caused by Fear

In Genesis 12, God calls one particular man to begin his plan of redemption. His name was Abram (later, Abraham).

The LORD had said to Abram, "Leave your native country, your relatives, and your father's family,

49

and go to the land that I will show you. I will make
you into a great nation. I will bless you and make
you famous, and you will be a blessing to others. I
will bless those who bless you and curse those who
treat you with contempt. All the families on earth
will be blessed through you." (Genesis 12:1–3)

Undoubtedly this was scary for Abram. He had to
leave his home, his country, and his relatives to go to an
unfamiliar foreign land. But Abram obeys; and follows
God's command.

So Abram departed as the Lord had instructed, and
Lot went with him. (Genesis 12:4)

Soon into the journey Abraham ran into his first obstacle. A severe famine struck the land of Canaan which
forced him to head further south to Egypt. As he was
approaching the border, he was concerned about his wife
Sarai (Sarah) and how the Egyptians would respond to
her beauty.

As he was approaching the border of Egypt, Abram
said to his wife, Sarai, "Look, you are a very beautiful woman. When the Egyptians see you, they will
say, 'This is his wife. Let's kill him; then we can have
her!' So please tell them you are my sister. Then they
will spare my life and treat me well because of their
interest in you." (Genesis 12:11–13)

Although God assured Abraham that he would bless
him with many descendants, Abraham was concerned
that the Egyptians might alter God's plan. Initially it

appeared that Abraham's scheme worked, at least in keeping him alive! As he and Sarah arrived in Egypt, everyone noticed Sarah's beauty and she was quickly escorted into the king's palace. Pharaoh was so taken with Sarah's beauty that he gave Abraham many gifts of animals and servants.

But the Lord intervened and sent terrible plagues upon Pharaoh because of Sarah. Soon the king was furious with Abraham for his deception and ordered he and Sarah to leave Egypt. God was faithful in protecting Abraham and Sarah even though they allowed their fear to manipulate the truth.

As Abraham and Sarah's journey continues, God promises to bless them with so many descendants that it would rival the stars in the sky (Genesis 15:5). But Abraham, perhaps blinded by fear again, decides to alter the truth a few chapters later while living in Gerar.

> While living there as a foreigner, Abraham introduced his wife, Sarah, by saying, "She is my sister." So King Abimelech of Gerar sent for Sarah and had her brought to him at his palace. (Genesis 20:2)

However, God proved to be faithful once again by warning Abimelech of his fate if he slept with Sarah. Abimelech was furious with Abraham! But Abraham responded:

> Abraham replied, "I thought, 'This is a godless place. They will want my wife and will kill me to get her.' And she really is my sister, for we both have the same father, but different mothers. And I married her. When God called me to leave my father's home and to travel from place to place, I told her,

51

'Do me a favor. Wherever we go, tell the people that
I am your brother.'" (Genesis 20:11–13)

Abimelech pays Abraham and Sarah for his unknowing,
wrongful intentions with gifts of animals, servants, and
1,000 pieces of silver. Once again, Abraham's blind spot
of fear didn't alter God's faithfulness and in the very next
chapter, God blesses Abraham and Sarah with the child
that had been promised.

The Blind Spot of Entitlement

Perhaps in the Old Testament there was no greater
king than David. He was not known for his large stature,
but his heart was huge for God. He didn't come from a
royal heritage, but rather humble beginnings, taking care
of his father's animals.

Then Samuel asked, "Are these all the sons you
have?" "There is still the youngest," Jesse replied.
"But he's out in the fields watching the sheep and
goats." (1 Samuel 16:11)

But despite his youth, God choose David to be the
next king of Israel. The hallmark of David's life was his
dependence on God and his faith that his God was faithful and powerful. Because of that unshakeable belief in
God's power, David killed Goliath, the Philistine giant
who was mocking God and threatening his people. The
current king Saul became jealous and tried to kill David
multiple times. But God protected David through these
battles and many more. Eventually David became the
king of Israel.

Is This a New Problem?

As long as David depended on God, his rule of Israel was blessed. Under his leadership, Israel was united, and her borders were expanding. The people of Israel experienced prosperity and David was cemented into their hearts as their king. But in that prosperity we found out that David's heart wandered from his dependence on God. And the result was a blind spot that caused great harm to himself and many others.

In the spring military battles usually resumed, but this year David sent his commander Joab and the Israelite army to fight the Ammonites without him. We don't know exactly why David chose to sit this battle out. Perhaps he was enjoying his accomplishments, but soon we learn that his leisure exposed a blind spot of epic proportions.

One afternoon, following a leisurely nap, David set out for a walk on the roof of his palace. Perhaps he was reflecting on his army's current victory while enjoying the cooler breezes of the late afternoon. After all, David's life had been filled with accomplishments. He had been loyal to God and God had blessed his faithfulness and humility. But David's life had not been easy up to this point. He had fought to earn the respect of the people of Israel, perhaps he was thinking that now he could enjoy the fruits of his labor.

Gazing over the city, he noticed a beautiful woman taking a bath. David's look led him to enquire about her identity. Her name was Bathsheba and she was the wife of Uriah the Hittite, who was a soldier in David's army. But that didn't deter David and he called his messengers to bring her to the palace. Despite knowing that her husband was currently engaged in combat, David engages in an adulterous affair, precipitating an avalanche of dreadful decisions. Soon after, she became pregnant and David began to develop a scheme to cover up his sin that eventually led to the murder of her husband Uriah.

It seems that David was completely blind to his sin. He had turned from God, taken another man's wife, and tried to cover up the resulting pregnancy with murder. That's an extreme example of what the blind spot of entitlement can do in our lives.

In the next chapter David's sin was exposed by Nathan the prophet. Nathan shares a story about a single beloved lamb taken from his poor master and killed for his dinner guests. David was outraged! Who would do such a thing? Isn't it interesting that David could easily see the blind spot of another? But not his own? But when Nathan connected the story to David's sin, his eyes were opened to what he had done. David turns to God in repentance and asks for forgiveness—really the best response when a blind spot has been exposed as sin (Psalm 51).

What started with an innocent look, led to an adulterous affair, and ended in a murder. David's story reminds us of the dangers of entitlement. Perhaps life is good and you have honored God along the way. Maybe you feel you've conquered the sinful temptations that dangerous blind spots can create. How quickly one look, one decision, or one entitled action can derail your life. Although God did forgive David, his sin still had terrible consequences for his child and his kingdom.

Drifting

These stories of blind spots make it clear that this is not a new problem. Throughout history, people have made decisions that have brought pain, suffering, and destruction. We yearn for a do-over, or at least the ability to prevent these disasters in the future.

All of these stories seem to have one common denominator. In each, the truth was distorted or ignored ever so slightly at first. What appeared to be a minor alteration at the beginning ultimately led to a path of destruction or at least pain and anguish. Blind spots cause us to drift from the truth.

So we must listen very carefully to the truth we have heard, or we may drift away from it. (Hebrews 2:1)

Blind spots start small, changing the narrative ever so slightly. Over time we lose sight of reality, which opens the door for all kinds of harmful behaviors to emerge from the shadows of our souls. Each sinful behavior creates distance from God even though God never steps away—the distance is always created by us. There have been times when I was not in a good place spiritually and I assumed God was giving me the cold shoulder. I thought that perhaps he needed some time to cool off from watching one of his children screw up. But that is not true, God remains faithful with his arms wide open. I believe there's no greater loss than allowing a sin or a blind spot to continue to create distance between you and your heavenly Father.

It is also critical to have a Nathan in our lives to expose our drifting. Often our drifting is so gradual we struggle to notice the change. Before we know it, the gap can appear to be an insurmountable challenge. But God can send Nathans into our lives to identify the drift if we are willing to listen. Just like a mirror can help identify a deadly blind spot while driving, a trusted friend can do the same for our spiritual lives. After all, what starts as a small speck can ultimately become a log in our eye, completely blocking our vision of the truth (Matthew 7:5)!

Ever since the serpent said, "Are you sure God said . . ." humankind has been tempted to drift from the truth. Know that God truly loves you. He sent his Son to pay the penalty of our sins so that we could be restored to a relationship to him. Because of his work, you can confess your blind spot and your sin to him to close the gap you have created. He will welcome you!

Be Encouraged

There are at least two ways to look at this chapter. First you may think, "Wow, I'm not alone. Many people before me have struggled with the same thing. What can I learn from these stories?" Or you may think, "Wow, blind spots have been around forever. I can't believe someone hasn't figured out how to avoid them. Perhaps there's no hope for me. I guess I'll continue to live my life hoping a blind spot doesn't cause a train wreck!"

It's much easier to recognize your blind spots when you see them in hindsight. But when you understand how blind spots develop, it gets easier to recognize them before they cause deep damage in your life. Stay focused on the truth. Watch for "serpents" that want to challenge God's plan for your life. Don't allow a sinful blind spot to cause you to compromise and rationalize a heart that is drifting from God. And when you see the blind spot, bring it to God for his forgiveness and his power to overcome it.

Get Engaged

Take a few minutes to consider ways you have drifted from the truth in what you believe and in how you are living your life. Maybe the gap still is small, so it seems harmless and insignificant at this point. Write down your original understanding of the truth and identify specific thoughts, behaviors, and attitudes that indicate that you are distancing yourself from it. Could it be a behavior a friend or spouse has recognized in you? Could it be an area of your life where you believe God might be disappointed in you? Remember, your heavenly Father never walks away. He stands with open arms to welcome you back to the truth! Bring what you have discovered to him for his forgiveness and help. Close the gap now to prevent a deadly blind spot from derailing your life.

CHAPTER 5

Seeing Ourselves and Others as Jesus Sees Us

Most merciful Redeemer, Friend and Brother, may
we know you more clearly, love you more dearly,
and follow you more nearly, day by day. Amen.
— Richard of Chichester's last words, 1253

(Fil)

Imagine that you and I are sitting together at an outdoor
café, talking about how we tend to view ourselves and
others. Assuming a high level of respect between us, we're
uncommonly truthful and honest. We agree that our
views of ourselves and others are always based on limited information. We also acknowledge our inability to
ever clearly see our own or other people's motives. Then
we begin distinguishing the likely differences between the
ways we view ourselves and others and Jesus's way of
viewing people.

I start by confessing a long-standing blind spot.
Often, I have assessed my value and other people's value

solely by what I'm able to see: personal achievements, acquisitions, and reputation. To illustrate my point, I take a $100 bill from my wallet. I ask, "Would you like this $100 to be yours?" Naturally, your enthusiastic, hopeful response is, "YES!" I then crumple the $100 bill and ask, "Do you still want it?" Your reply is obviously, "Yes."

Next, I put the $100 on the sidewalk and grind it with my shoe. "Do you want it now?" I ask. "Absolutely" you reply. You understand that whatever I do to the $100 bill will not decrease its value. It will still be worth $100.

Lots of times people get crumpled, stepped on, kicked, and ground into the dirt because of personal decisions and those made by others. Sometimes there's no apparent explanation for the difficult circumstances a person confronts in life. Regardless of the cause, though, the effect is often that we view ourselves and others with contempt, as less, even worthless.

This is the radical difference between how we tend to view ourselves and others and Jesus's way of seeing people. No matter what has happened or what will happen, from Jesus's perspective, our value will never be diminished. Dirty or clean, crumpled or nicely creased, Jesus views us as priceless.

Looking vs. Seeing

A wise and compassionate pastor once said that if we who teach and preach had X-ray vision to look into the hearts of the people sitting before us, we would break down and weep.

I try to keep this in mind whenever I speak to a group of people. My hope is always that some of the people feel good about their lives. They are the picture of health, with great jobs and happy home lives; they have ample reason to be pleased with the way life is going.

I suspect that there are always others who are struggling, feeling weary, disappointed, frustrated, angry, or afraid. Life just isn't going their way. They feel like they're on an emotional roller-coaster that seems to never stop long enough to get off. They feel vulnerable, up-for-grabs, as if their life is out of control.

And although I wish it weren't so, it's likely that some are in a dark, stormy season of life. They feel that their life isn't worth much; they have no reason to hope it's going to get better. Thinking that God has abandoned them, they see their life as broken beyond repair. Feeling that there's nothing left to live for, they're losing hope that life will ever change.

What about your life? Which of these groups do you identify with most? Regardless of your answer, I can assure you that Jesus sees and understands our natural condition. We are born spiritually blind, lost, and separated from God. That's why Jesus came. His mission is to expose the deadly nature of our spiritual blindness and help us to see that he alone has the cure.

Too often, the busyness of our lives prevents us from truly seeing. We observe an accident while traveling, but do we know the harm to the people involved? We glance at a husband and wife straining to appear healthy, but do we see the fractures in the foundation of their marriage? We look at a timid girl, eating alone in the middle school lunchroom, but do we know the aching in her heart for friends?

Jesus Sees a Man Born Blind

The apostle John devotes an entire chapter to the story of Jesus healing a man who was born blind (John 9).

This account is about more than a miracle; it's also about what Jesus sees that we tend to miss. Jesus recognizes the challenges, limitations, and liabilities associated with our spiritual blindness, the way it immobilizes, misleads, and cripples, creating guilt and shame, anger and bitterness, worry and regret, fear and anxiety.

In contrast, Jesus has a unique way of seeing all things, and he wants us to see ourselves and others as he sees us. He wants us to see that the man blind from birth represents every man and every woman. His blindness represents the "sin of the world" which "the Lamb of God takes away" (John 1:29). By nature, we are all blind until our eyes are opened by Christ, who is "the Light of the world" (John 8:12; 9:5).

A Picture Worth 1,000 Words

For centuries Jesus's followers have seen the story of the man born blind as a metaphor for the human condition apart from Christ. It vividly expresses the work of Christ. As the story progresses, the healed man's understanding of Jesus gradually grows from "the man called Jesus" (9:11), to "a prophet" (v. 17), and then a man "from God" (v. 33), to "the Son of Man" (vv. 35–36). Finally, the man acknowledges, "Lord, I believe," and worships Jesus (v. 38).

While the man born blind advances gradually toward fuller and clearer sight, both physically and spiritually, the presumptuously "all-seeing" religious leader's blindness becomes more inexplicably apparent. By the end of the story Jesus explains that he entered the world, ". . . to give sight to the blind and to show those who think they see that they are blind" (John 9:39). Their response shows that they are incredulous: "Are you saying we're blind?" (John 9:40). Jesus's reply is decisive, "If you were blind, you wouldn't be guilty. But you remain guilty because you claim you can see" (John 9:41). In other words, "If you just admitted that you don't have it altogether, that you sometimes don't see clearly and that you need help, your uncertainty about yourself would be an admission of your need for me."

The story begins. "As Jesus was walking along, he saw a man who had been blind from birth" (John 9:1). I imagine the day began like any other. The blind man occupied his usual spot by the side of the road on the outskirts of Jerusalem. Once settled, he started crying out, "Alms for the blind!" This daily ritual was his only means of survival. Begging was his specialized occupation. While many walked past him, occasionally tossing a coin his way, very few truly saw him. For most, he had become a blind spot, someone they ignored or didn't even notice as they walked along the road.

On this day, he could tell that the road was unusually crowded. It was a religious holiday, the Feast of Tabernacles, when Jewish people were to gather in Jerusalem. The blind beggar was likely hoping for a spike in revenue with a massive crowd pouring in. Perhaps some pilgrims would notice him for a change and demonstrate some kindness.

Most people assumed that his blindness was God's punishment for someone's sin. This was a common explanation. Rabbis even taught that children could commit sins in their mother's womb.

The blind beggar wasn't the only one in the crowd with heightened senses. Jesus had them too. The sight of this unwanted, excluded beggar captured Jesus's attention. Perhaps Jesus was feeling especially attuned to this man after a painful discussion he and his disciples had recently had with the Jewish authorities. Perhaps it heightened Jesus's awareness of what it felt like to be unwanted and excluded, like the blind beggar.

As Jesus and his followers approach him, the blind man overhears a question that people have always asked: "Rabbi . . . why was this man born blind? Was it because of his sins or his parents' sins?" There is no room for doubt: Someone has done something wrong. "There is no death without sin, and there is no suffering without iniquity,"[1] taught the Pharisees, who believed that natural disasters, congenital disabilities, and long-term conditions like paralysis and blindness were punishments from God.

In his book *The Jesus I Never Knew,* author Philip Yancey offers this astute observation:

> I have noticed a remarkable change since Jesus' time in how people think about calamity. Nowadays we tend to blame God, both for the cataclysmic (which insurance companies call "acts of God") and for the trivial. At the 1994 Winter Olympics, when speed-skater Dan Janssen scraped the ice and lost the 500-meter race once again, his wife, Robin, cried out instinctively, "Why, God, again? God can't be that cruel!" A few months later a young woman wrote Dr. James Dobson this letter: "Four years ago, I was dating a man and became pregnant. I was devastated! I asked God, 'Why have You allowed this to happen to me?'" Exactly what role, I cannot help but wonder, did God play in an ice-skater losing control on a turn and a young couple losing control on a date?[2]

Some things never seem to change. I sadly recall church leaders attributing the Haiti earthquake disaster to the Haitians' sin of voodoo worship. I suspect that in much—perhaps in most—of what happens in life, it's best for us to leave cause and effect in God's hands. I recall the wisdom of Dr. Dale Bruner, scholar in residence at Fuller Seminary, saying that the only satisfactory answers to our questions about the endless problems of evil ("Why does God . . . ?" "How can a loving God . . . ?") will come from Jesus Christ and him alone when he returns. Bruner added that Jesus himself, in his utter humanity, asked from the cross, "Why?" (Matthew 27:46; Mark 15:34). If Jesus asked this question, so may we. However, it also behooves us to recall that Jesus received no answer for three long days. It shouldn't surprise us when we don't get an answer until our life ends.

Cause vs. Cure

Jesus responded to his disciples' question by invalidating the prevailing notion about God's view of sick and disabled people. His answer was a flat denial that the man's blindness was due to any sin, just as he overturned the notion that tragedies only occur to those who deserve them (see Luke 13:1–5). "It was not because of his sins or his parents' sins," Jesus answered. "This happened so the power of God could be seen in him" (John 9:3).

The disciples were curious about the cause, while Jesus focused on the cure and the good that could come from it. This man and his parents, of course, had sinned like all other human beings, but Jesus made clear that their sin was not the reason for his blindness. This man's blindness occurred, Jesus says, so that in his healing and in his response to Christ, God's gracious power could become community news.

Here's Mud in Your Eye

Without any warning, the blind beggar felt someone smear a thick muddy paste across his eyes. Perhaps it was best that he couldn't see that it was Jesus's spit mixed with some dirt. Jesus's hands-on approach inspires me. He touches the man. Jesus heals not only with his words but also through his touch. Touch is the first and foremost of our five senses. It conveys love because it demonstrates presence and tenderness. A baby needs touch to live and grow healthy. A sick person needs compassion in order to trust. Kindness never hurts or destroys the weak and the vulnerable. It reveals to them their value and beauty. It implies respect.

Here's a fascinating detail I suspect Jesus wants us to see. Again, my friend Dale Bruner offers this scholarly insight.

"On *his* eyes" is the most accurate translation explaining where Jesus placed the mud. This is the first of nine uses of the word "eyes" in John 9 (vv. 6, 10, 11, 14, 15, 17, 21, 26, 30). In all nine cases, the word "eyes" has a personal pronoun accompanying it, as here, and all nine times the pronoun is elevated by being placed outside its natural order in Greek and is placed decisively *before* the word.

It is as if our author is saying, "Jesus smeared the mud in *his* eyes; readers, what about *your* eyes?" In other words, Jesus is asking us through John's telling of the story, "Have *your* eyes been touched?"

Then, the kind yet commanding voice of the Rabbi gives the blind man clear and simple instructions: "'Go wash yourself in the pool of Siloam.' . . . So the man went and washed and came back seeing!" (John 9:7).

Onlookers who had previously ignored him now led the blind man down the hill to the pool. After what they witnessed, they were glad to give their assistance. Splashing water on his face and wiping the mud away, he saw the light for the first time in his life. Overwhelmed with joy, he ran home, navigating for the first time with his newly sighted eyes.

Those of us who have always had our vision can't know how beautiful it must be to have sight. But this man isn't the only one who has spent a lifetime near something without seeing it. We all suffer some form of blindness. We can live next to something for a lifetime, but unless we take time to focus on it, it doesn't become a part of our life. Unless we have our blindness lifted, we live in a world of blind spots.

What began as a dreadful saga of a man's blindness ends as a surreal revelation of everyone else's blindness. His neighbors and others who knew him seem flabbergasted and confused. "'Isn't this the man who used to sit and beg?' Some said he was, and others said, 'No, he just looks like him!'" (John 9:8–9).

This man has been overlooked and ignored by his neighbors to such an extent that they're not sure who he is! I suspect that, growing up, this man had never been invited to a friend's house to play or go to a party. He'd never been invited to enjoy the companionship of a group of friends.

Now, soon after his blind eyes are healed, he gets his first real look at the ugly, harmful effects of the worst form of blindness—spiritual blindness. It's not entirely clear why his neighbors take him to the Pharisees, who subject him to a formal interrogation about the "alleged sinner" who healed his blindness. Perhaps it was customary to have them analyze unusual occurrences. Maybe they wanted, or needed, their theological assessment. Conceivably they hoped the Pharisees would be impressed by the incredible event. In any case and in the midst of this process, his parents plead ignorance, fearing the consequences of guilt by association. But the healed man is not intimidated. Pressed for details about who healed him, he tells them the one thing he knows for certain. "'I don't know whether he is a sinner,' the man replied. 'But I know this: I was blind and now I can see!'" (John 9:25).

The reason for this drama is that in Jerusalem, where Jesus had been labeled a heretic by the Pharisees, a miracle on the Sabbath was a major violation. While saving a life on the Sabbath was allowed, the treatment of other ailments was reserved for workdays. By healing the man born blind, Jesus had crossed that line.

Telling the truth about his healing didn't sit well with the Pharisees, so they threw the man out of the synagogue. There's an extreme irony here. While the religious leaders were scandalized that Jesus has "worked" on the day they were commanded to rest, they were working their tails off trying to verify that Jesus had been working.

When Jesus heard about this, he immediately found the man and asked him a question whose answer would forever change the trajectory of his life.

"Do you believe in the Son of Man?"

The man answered, "Who is he, sir? I want to believe in him."

"You have seen him," Jesus said, "and he is speaking to you!"

"Yes, Lord, I believe!" the man said. And he worshiped Jesus. (vv. 35–38)

67

It's only speculation, but it's easy to imagine that the man would later tell his friends, "My eyes worked for the first time in my life, and the first person I saw was the Messiah. It was the best day of my life!"

Meanwhile, blinded by their limited, rigid interpretation of Scripture, and their fear of the threat Jesus posed to their reputation and power, the Pharisees refused to see the truth. For them, the truth was a blind spot.

There are lots of blind spots in this story, so let's go back and consider a few.

Someone We Are *Incapable of Seeing*

Recently our older son and his wife attended a Good Friday service that our younger son was leading. As our younger son welcomed the crowd, his sister-in-law anxiously asked her husband, "Where is your brother?"

Puzzled by her question, her husband replied, "He's standing directly in front of you, extending a warm welcome to you." Since the last time they'd been together, our younger son had buzzed his head and shaved his winter beard. He looked nothing like the person she expected to see.

A blind spot may be someone or something we are incapable of seeing because of our expectations or bias. That's why the Pharisees were unable to recognize Jesus. Their certainty about the rightness of their convictions about the Messiah made it impossible for them to see who he truly was even when he stood before them. When a supernatural miracle confronted them, they could not—would not—make the connection between the miracle and the Miracle Man Jesus. Instead, they ran an investigation, questioning every possible suspect and witness to prove themselves correct. When the truth confronted them, they resorted to insults, intimidation, and expulsion. Their blind spot made them unable to see.

Jesus is a bright light shining in the world today. And whenever light flashes, it creates both brightness and shadows. Jesus's invasion of our planet immediately created division. Nobody remained neutral. The Pharisees illustrate how we can become extremely rigid in following rules and wind up in the shadows rather than in the light. To them, Jesus was a blinding light. They preferred to blindly follow the god they imagined rather than see the Light of God who created them.

Someone We *Refuse to See*

Fear blinded the blind man's parents. There's not even a trace of happiness that their son can see them for the first time! Anxiety about losing their good standing in the synagogue eclipses all other concerns.

Do you have blind spots due to worry and fear? Are there people you neglect seeing because of possible consequences, perhaps someone who has hurt, betrayed, or been a burden to you?

What if Jesus says to you, "It's time for you to open your eyes and remove this blind spot"? If you are willing to look, you might discover why they are this way. It might enable you to see them as Jesus sees them.

Currently, there is a person in the spotlight who "rubs my fur the wrong way." It's challenging for me to love them. At least until recently, when I began wondering, "Who hurt you? To me, you appear to have a deep wound, and I feel sad for you."

Someone We *Avoid Seeing*

Perhaps those who passed the blind man on the side of the road avoided him for the same reason I sometimes change lanes when approaching a stop light and see a disheveled person with a cardboard sign. I'm somewhat like the disciples. I ponder and debate the causes of injustice and oppression, homelessness and malnutrition, racism and sexism, rather than address the needs they produce. I rehearse questions about who's responsible or who's to blame. Sometimes I don't see people and their needs that are right in front of me, because I've grown accustomed to their existence or because I just don't want to see. Sadly, I confess, some of those people are those with whom I share a last name, and even the same house.

Being Seen by Jesus

Several years ago, while my family was enjoying a week on the North Carolina coast, I took a walk alone down a crowded beach. After walking quite a distance, I noticed a young, darkly tanned boy playing in the shallow surf. I'd guess he was about nine years old. He was having what appeared to be the time of his life. While watching him splash and squeal, I remember thinking, "Pal, you are redefining my concept of fun!" Standing twenty or thirty yards away, he suddenly turned and our eyes met. It wasn't a casual glance; our eyes locked. It was a magical moment. As I looked, I could see that he had Down's syndrome. At that moment his innocent face burst into a gigantic smile, and he began screaming what might have been a name, though I could not understand what he was squealing. Perhaps it was the name of someone he mistook me for. Suddenly, our eyes still locked in on each other, he began running toward me with his arms wide open. I admit I panicked a little, but without time to sort out how to best respond, I knelt down and opened my arms as he ran into them. With his arms wrapped tightly around my neck, he began kissing me wildly on my lips. After what felt like forever, he loosened his grip, tilted his head back, and with his blue eyes riveted on mine, his face burst again into a smile. I will remember that moment for the rest of my life.

By that time a woman with a worried expression was standing beside us. She tried to apologize, and I assured her that all was well.

Moments later I was once again walking alone down the crowded beach. When I returned to my family and began telling my wife about the encounter, I said, "Honey, he hugged and kissed me like I've never been hugged and kissed before."

For the next several days I couldn't escape the power of that experience. Still, I was not certain why this encounter had so dramatically impacted my life. Finally, a few evenings later, sitting alone on our front porch, God spoke to me. "Fil, I'd love to tell you why that encounter has such a grip on you. That little boy was a picture of my wild and reckless love for you. The way he looked into your eyes is the way I have always looked at you. That beaming smile on his face is how you make me smile. The way he wildly screamed with glee is how I feel about you. The way he held you in that tight embrace is like mine. The way he kissed you only begins to convey the love that is in my heart for you. Fil, you can't imagine how great and infinite is the love in my heart for you. I am crazy about you. I can't take my eyes off you."

Even now as I write about that encounter, my eyes are flooded with tears. I haven't been the same since, nor will I ever be. The love of Jesus Christ has forever changed me! It is one thing to know something in your head and quite another when it makes its way down into your heart.

Being seen by Jesus, having our eyes open to him, is how our eyes are opened to others. It's the love of God flowing through us that gives us eyes of love and compassion for those around us. Instead of seeing only our own needs, we are open to seeing others. For the remainder of my life, I want to see others the way Jesus sees me.

Be Encouraged

My desire—and perhaps it's your desire too—is to love Jesus more dearly, to see him more clearly, to follow him more nearly, day by day. However, I know that I still have blind spots. I need Jesus's help to see what I tend to miss.

John ends his story with Jesus's concluding challenge:

"I entered this world to render judgment—to give sight to the blind and to show those who think they see that they are blind." (John 9:39)

The blind beggar's healing challenges us to admit that we have blind spots that prevent us from seeing what Jesus sees. We need Jesus to show us how to see what we tend to miss.

Get Engaged

First, take some time to settle down, relax, and open yourself to the possibility of seeing yourself as Jesus sees you. Rest in the freedom that comes with knowing that Jesus loves you as you are, not as you should be, since none of us will ever be the person we should be. That is why Jesus came to give his life for us.

Next, read this modern paraphrase of Romans 8:38–39.

God, I may fall flat on my face; I may fail until I feel old and beaten and done in. Yet Your goodness and love is changeless. All the music may go out of my life; my private world may shatter to dust. Even so, You hold me in the palm of Your steady hand. No turn in the affairs of my fractured life can baffle You. Satan with all his braggadocio cannot distract You. Nothing can separate me from Your measureless love—pain can't, disappointment can't, anguish can't. Yesterday, today, tomorrow can't. The loss of my dearest love can't. Death can't, life can't. Riots, wars, insanity, non-identity, hunger, neurosis, disease—none of these things, nor all of them heaped together—can budge the fact that I am dearly loved, completely forgiven and forever free through Jesus Christ, Your beloved Son.[3]

The focus of this chapter has been seeing ourselves and others as Jesus sees us, and how being seen, loved, and changed by Jesus opens our eyes and hearts to ourselves and others.

- How open are your eyes to God's unconditional love for you?
- How open are your eyes to God's unconditional love for others?

Ask Jesus to guide you through the remainder of today with this truth fixed in your mind: "You are dearly loved, completely forgiven, and forever free through Jesus Christ."

CHAPTER 6

What Jesus Says about Seeing and Speaking the Truth

An open rebuke is better than hidden love! Wounds from a sincere friend are better than many kisses from an enemy. (Proverbs 27:5–6)

(Fil)

A Bittersweet Memory

Last summer, our family spent a week vacationing on the North Carolina coast. One evening while strolling to our favorite spot to watch the sunset, I made a nonchalant, innocent (to me, at least) remark that was intended only for fun. Nonetheless, for the remainder of the evening, I detected a sharp edge in several comments my daughter directed to me.

The next morning, when I cautiously asked her whether there was a problem, I received a stern "Yes!" And a stream of tears began pouring down her precious, sad face.

I could see that I had wounded my daughter, whom I cherish. "Would you please tell me what I did that hurt you? Honestly, I don't have a clue."

I didn't have to ask twice. My daughter led me out the front door and down the stairs. Walking briskly ahead of me, she headed toward the shore. When we were alone, she began unpacking her feelings about the hurtful thing I had said. My heart was suddenly and sadly broken, as hers had been since the previous evening.

Her kindness was overwhelming. Giving me the benefit of the doubt, she acknowledged my innocence and expressed confidence that I had intended no malice. Nonetheless, for good reason, she had been deeply hurt by what I said.

Want to know the cause of the hurt I inflicted on my daughter? Sadly, it was a blind spot.

My regret was apparent. I humbly expressed my remorse and sadness, and asked for forgiveness. Then I thanked my daughter for being so open and honest. She graciously obliged.

Looking back on that bittersweet memory, I cherish my daughter's loving courage to say what others might choose to keep to themselves. Her fierce devotion to what is right and proper exposed my blind spot.

I can't help wondering, can you relate? If so, in what ways?

Why Aren't We More Honest?

To appreciate how beautiful this moment was, think of how *rarely* it occurs, and how, even *more* rarely, exposing another's blind spot is done well. Most people live their entire lives without anyone, ever, speaking honest, loving, direct words to the most consequential problems in their lives. Pause for a moment and count the times this has been done for you. Better yet, count the times you've offered this to someone you love.

75

Instead, we make small talk and we chit-chat. We spend our days half-heartedly engaging in conversations as substantive as a puff of smoke. When there's tension, conflict, or hurt inflicted, we dance around each other like birds in a mating ritual; ducking, bobbing, sticking out our chests, flapping our wings, ruffling up our feathers, circling one another, advancing and retreating. We're like something you see on *Planet Earth*.

I believe that lovingly speaking the truth is the most neglected, the most misunderstood, the least practiced, and the most needed communication in the body of Christ. So, for crying out loud, why *aren't* we more honest with each other?

I'll admit my primary reasons, at least those I'm able to see. Sometimes I weigh the cost/benefit ratio and decide it's just too expensive. I've risked being truthful often enough to know that honesty often costs more than it pays. And I'll admit, sometimes I'm a coward.

As I dig deeper into my motives, I also realize I don't always care enough. Instead, I choose to ignore or deny upsetting things until they settle down or go away. I don't care enough to risk the awkwardness, tension, backlash, penalties, or rejection that frequently comes with telling the sometimes hard and painful truth.

But in reality these things don't eventually go away. Instead, they get bottled up inside me, fermenting, building pressure. When the cork pops, like a bottle of champagne, what comes out is nothing like sparkling wine. Instead, it's bitter and stinking of irritation, exasperation, resentment, or anger.

Disruptive Honesty

That's why I admire and desire Jesus's courageous, loving, disruptive honesty. He shoots straight. Sometimes he's playful, sometimes fierce; the next moment he's tender or generous. Jesus's disruptive honesty is indispensable because you can rely on him to offer it in the best possible way for you to hear it.

Jesus not only tells the truth, he embodies it. Truth is not just what he offers us; it's his identity. He says, "I am the way, *the truth*, and the life" (John 14:6 emphasis added). When Jesus calls himself the truth, it's helpful to keep in mind the Greek notion of truth. Truth means that the veil that lies over reality is taken away and we see truth as it is.

This is the reason why blind spots are so hurtful; they prevent us from seeing reality. Either we don't see the truth at all, or we see it as if it were under a veil. Often the veil is one that we've drawn over our lives because what it's covering is unacceptable, perhaps shameful to us. We fear it will be unacceptable to others too. Those who try to run away from the truth about themselves or hide it are typically afraid that the truth will catch up with them and others will discover what lies behind their façade.

Jesus has the ability and desire to take away this veil that prevents us from seeing reality. God's Spirit is the great unmasker of our blind spots. Jesus is the only one who can expose our blind spots without utterly destroying us.

When we walk with Jesus and allow his truth to work its way into our lives, Jesus says that this truth makes us free. He could have added that sometimes it will make us miserable before it makes us free. Facing our blind spots is occasionally frightening and painful, primarily when they are covering our guilt and shame. To a certain extent, they have served us by protecting us. But their protection is a dreadful illusion (John 8:31–36).

77

Think about this before reading any further: "How beneficial would it be to have someone in your life who knows you intimately, loves you regardless, and is willing to be completely honest with you about your blind spots? It would be a little unsettling and undoubtedly disruptive—but doesn't part of you also crave it?"

The best, the dearest, and the most profound friendships I have had have one thing in common: each person has loved me enough to put our friendship on the line and tell me things about my life that no one else cared enough to say.

The more we realize that this loving, kind, disruptive honesty is what we need, the more we'll fall in love with Jesus for the way he provides it. We'll be open to receive it and less afraid to offer it to the people we love.

Where Are We Headed?

Here's an example of disruptive honesty. "One day Jesus left the crowds to pray alone. Only his disciples were with him, and he asked them, 'Who do people say I am?' 'Well,' they replied, 'Some say John the Baptist, some say Elijah, and others say you are one of the other ancient prophets risen from the dead'" (Luke 9:18–19).

Until now, Jesus and his companions had been having a friendly, engaging conversation, although I suspect his question caught some of them off guard. Jesus then takes them to a deeper, more intimate, and personally relevant place in their exchange.

"But who do *you* say I am?"

Then Peter, either divinely inspired or simply intuitively, spoke up. "You are the Messiah sent from God" (Luke 9:20).

Right on the heels of Peter's declaration, Jesus makes a startling prediction of his death. "The Son of Man must suffer many terrible things," he said. "He will be rejected by the elders, the leading priests, and the teachers of religious law. He will be killed, but on the third day he will be raised from the dead" (v. 22).

When Mark tells his version of this story, he adds a fascinating exchange between Peter and Jesus. "Peter took him aside and began to reprimand him for saying such things" (Mark 8:32). Peter "reprimands" Jesus?! That's a harsh word indicating Peter's strong emotional reaction to Jesus's prediction.

Then, as if what Jesus had told them about himself wasn't shocking enough, Jesus goes on to say, "If any of you wants to be my follower, you must give up your own way, take up your cross daily, and follow me. If you try to hang on to your life, you will lose it. But if you give up your life for my sake, you will save it" (Luke 9:23–24).

It's like Jesus is saying, "I don't want you, friends, to have a blind spot about this. It's essential that you understand where this journey is going to take us. Friends, your world is about to change drastically. Where we're headed is going to cost you everything that you hold dear."

What Jesus is saying to his closest friends is like the young lady who told her boyfriend, "Look, you better know how needy I am. You better put your track shoes on and run away from me as fast as you can, before we fall any more in love. If you marry me, you're going to have a hard life."

His decisive response: "I'm staying."

What that young lady did is precisely what Jesus is doing here. He's saying, "I know you're falling in love with me, but you'd better know where this is going to lead you. I'm giving you your track shoes right now. You can run, but if you keep falling in love with me, it's going to lead you to death. It's going to lead you to lose everything that matters most to you and that the world says is important. You'd be wise to decide now: Do you want to stay?"

The accounts of Luke and the other Gospel writers still apply to us thousands of years later, but when those authors recorded their accounts, they were thinking of the needs of their audiences then and there. Luke wanted to help his readers to live better lives and to answer the questions that were troubling them.

As far as we can tell, Luke was probably writing a manual for missionaries who were going out on a mission from his community. He crafted his message for the training, cultivation, and emotional support of missionaries. To be effective, these new followers of Jesus needed to understand themselves—their identity, goals, and problems—before they went out.

What Does Jesus Know?

Some people today might question, "How could someone who lived over two thousand years ago in a radically different culture have anything meaningful or relevant to say about the threats that our twenty-first-century blind spots pose? How might his strangely different life intersect with our own? Who does Jesus think he is? In other words, how could Jesus Christ, a carpenter from Nazareth who claimed to be God, have any insight into our lives today?"

This is my answer. Jesus understands more than we do about human life—all the messy realities and challenges of being human. He still understands. Jesus wasn't God merely pretending to be human. He *was* human. He got hungry. He ate and drank. He got tired and sleepy. The physical realities of human life that we face confronted Jesus too.

As a fully human person, Jesus felt the entire range of human emotions. He could be, for instance, light-hearted. The fact that children wanted to be near him is ample proof that being with him felt safe and fun. He had a sense of humor, as indicated by the amusing characters in the stories he told. He was even comical, since he seemed to enjoy giving nicknames to some of his followers. For instance, he named Peter "Rock" for his (eventual) stability, and called James and John "Sons of Thunder" for their tempers.

Jesus experienced the more challenging emotions and allowed us to be witnesses to them. He could grow agitated, even annoyed at times. He said to the disciples at one point, "You people are too stubborn to have any faith! How much longer must I be with you? Why do I have to put up with you?" (Matthew 17:17 CEV). He wept over his friend Lazarus's death. He endured life-crushing agony in the Garden of Gethsemane. These are just a few recounted incidents.

There are other emotions reflected in his life too. Jesus loved his earthly parents, Mary and Joseph; he cared about the members of his extended family, and valued meaningful friendships with a wide range of people.

Jesus also understood the challenge of work. He didn't merely waltz onto the world stage at the start of his strategic mission, having spent the previous thirty years praying and drifting aimlessly through life without a care in the world. Besides the daily chores of helping his family run a household, he probably spent half of those years working as Joseph's assistant. Jesus was a worker who led a fully human emotional, physical, mental, and spiritual life.

Because Jesus is also fully God, he knew that the deadliest blind spot entered human hearts and history when our first parents, Adam and Eve, believed the lie that they would be *like* God *without* God. Jesus knew that without God, the most that Adam, Eve, and all of their descendants could ever do was make ourselves into our own false gods. Jesus knew that all of our blind spots would be the outgrowth of Adam and Eve's fatal error. At the same time, because Jesus was fully human, he suffered in the midst of the messy and beautiful experience of being human. In the drudgery and fulfillment of his working life, Jesus witnessed the devastating effects of sin and spiritual blindness in the lives of the people he encountered.

A Crucial Challenge

Jesus came to earth to fulfill a crucial, monumental mission. The task would cost him his life. For centuries, his human brothers and sisters had lived in spiritual darkness that prevented them from seeing what's true about God, others, and themselves. Jesus came here to be God's light to illuminate our dark, skeptical, broken human souls. He came to open people's eyes to help them see the destruction that threatened their lives and, in his death, to pay the penalty that would set them free.

Often Jesus chose to open people's spiritual eyes using stories he called "parables." Knowing our hearts and minds perfectly and understanding the nature of blind spots, Jesus chose an approach from his Jewish heritage. Inspired by the examples of the ancient prophets, Jesus told parables to help his audience listen to the hard-to-swallow truth. What the proverb was to Solomon and the Psalms to God's people at prayer, these stories were to Jesus's mission of reconciliation.

One day his disciples asked Jesus, "Why do you tell stories?"

His response suggests that he'd been hoping someone would ask. "I tell stories to create readiness, to nudge the people toward receptive insight. In their present state, they can stare till doomsday and not see it, listen till they're blue in the face and not get it" (Matthew 13:13 MSG). His response, quoting the prophet Isaiah, indicates how keenly aware Jesus is of our blind spots and the threats they pose.

> "Your ears are open but you don't hear a thing.
> Your eyes are awake but you don't see a thing.
> The people are blockheads!
> They stick their fingers in their ears
>   so they don't have to listen;
> They screw their eyes shut
>   so they don't have to look,
> so they don't have to deal with me face-to-face
> and let me heal them." (Matthew 13:14–15 MSG)

Jesus proceeded to tell them how fortunate they were to have "God-blessed eyes—eyes that see."

Intriguing and engaging plots characterized Jesus's stories. They drew people into their drama, lowering their defenses and opening a way for new insights to capture their minds and hearts.

Perhaps the most distinctive characteristic of Jesus's parables was the element of surprise. Just when his listeners thought a parable was about someone else, it turned out to be about them! His parables often began as portraits, and then suddenly turned into mirrors in which people saw things about themselves that they had not seen before.

It was a brilliant technique, executed with compassionate and loving finesse. People came running to

Jesus experiencing all types of fear, trauma, and anger. Rather than confronting them head-on and driving them deeper into their defensiveness, he defused their anxiety by saying, "Let me tell you a story." Then, drawn in by the narrative and with their defenses down, his listeners would see themselves in the story. Their spiritual blind spot was exposed, enabling them to see what Jesus had always seen.

The themes in Jesus's parables reflect the heart of his teaching. Certain parables illustrate the grace and kindness of God in forgiving us though we don't deserve it. Other stories depict the sternness of God when we refuse his mercy. Some of Jesus's parables stress the importance of obedience, even though it can never make us worthy of his love, while others show that God is not interested in appearances but in the hidden, inner qualities of our hearts. Jesus's stories often point to the inestimable value of our adoption as daughters and sons in his kingdom. Other teachings focus on the spiritual and universal nature of God's kingdom. Another highlight of Jesus's parables is that what may seem weak, small, and insignificant from the world's perspective is most important in God's overall economy.

Jesus's three years of engaging humanity is a strategic values intervention. Jesus is on a mission to wake people up to the reality of their spiritual blindness and need for redemption. The gentleness or severity of his truth-telling is measured out with great care, according to the amount of delusion and self-deception that's controlling his listener. When a soul is captured by pride, bigotry, self-righteousness, and intellectual or social elitism—among the many blind spots he confronts—Jesus strikes with skill and precision.

You Can't Do This All Alone

Over two decades ago I was introduced to a group of unruly Christ followers who call themselves "the Notorious Sinners." These men come from across the country and from all walks of life. They meet once a year to authentically share their untidy lives with each other. The title Notorious Sinners refers to the scandalous category of forgiven sinners whose reputations and ongoing flaws didn't seem to keep Jesus away. Jesus had a habit of attracting and befriending disreputable folks; he called them disciples. He still does. I like people who are open and committed to identifying their blind spots. Graciously, these men invited me to be part of their group.

The Notorious Sinners usually get together at a spiritual retreat center, where from the moment we arrive, we run the risk of being viewed with suspicion by the center's leadership. I suspect this has something to do with our moniker. We also don't act like people who typically come to these kinds of places—reserved, quiet, silently seeking the voice of God (although that's who we hope to hear).

One of the Notorious Sinners, now deceased, was author Mike Yaconelli, who offered this pithy portrayal: "We're earthy, boisterous, noisy, and rowdy, tramping around our souls seeking God, hanging out with a rambunctious Jesus who is looking for a good time in our hearts."[1]

I Need All the Help I Can Get

I need these men, and others like them, in my life; men whose devotion to Jesus is unashamedly real and wildly passionate, characterized by brazen godliness. Unafraid to admit their blind spots, unintimidated by

Christ followers who deny their messiness, these men sometimes look like they're far from Jesus and at other times they look just like him. They are spiritual rabble-rousers, which is why they look like Jesus (who himself caused a stir a time or two). They are full of playfulness, laughter, and boisterous behavior, which is why they look like pagans. (Jesus was also accused of such things.)

Several years ago, Mike was our host. The night before my scheduled departure for the retreat, there was a massive crisis in our family. My response was outrageously shameful and ungodly. But when I called the group to explain my predicament, emphasizing that it "involved one of our children," I presented myself as heroic and self-sacrificing, dutiful even, for choosing to make the sacrifice to remain at home.

Months later, when he and I were together, Mike demonstrated the skill of a surgeon as he laid me open, exposing the truth that I was confident had remained hidden. "Dude, I know why you didn't come, and it wasn't because your family needed you. It was your excessive, stinking pride! You knew that if you remained at home, it would appear that your family crisis was entirely about them and they needed you to fix it. Man, you may have fooled them, but not me. Your pride is an enormous blind spot, and I see it as bright as day!"

What happened next was the most transforming part of the whole experience. Inwardly, I met Mike's well-intentioned remarks with rejection, denial, and hostility. It was all I could do to contain my prideful rage. I was about to explode when I saw tears in his eyes, and his lips began to quiver. He stood up and made his way toward me. Sitting down beside me, he asked with tender kindness, "Fil, what will it take for you to stop being controlled by your fear of being useless and unable to help? Won't you please stop hiding and let yourself be known? When you let others see the real you, then and only then will you experience the love for which you've always yearned."

On numerous occasions, I'd been awestruck as Mike offered to large crowds the words he was now personally directing toward me. "Fil, accepting the reality of our broken, flawed lives is the starting point of living with Jesus, not because living with Jesus will mend our brokenness, but because we then stop seeking perfection. Instead, we seek Jesus, the one who is present in the brokenness of our lives."

Mike had exposed what I suspect is my most enormous, debilitating blind spot: *pride*. In doing so, he helped me see that much of my giving and caring had been motivated by my own subconscious needs for love and esteem; which was the opposite of how I saw myself. Through this humiliation, I've seen a decline in my compulsion to help whenever I see a need. I'm freer to say no and to accept that my assistance isn't always needed or wanted. Surrendering my constant need to be needed has enabled me to experience more humility, pure love, and sincere generosity. I'm more able to receive love from God and others without trying to earn it by helping. It's also opened me up to the value of seeing what's hidden in my blind spots.

A Special Kind of Care

Mike's bold but loving care for me is the kind described by the renowned priest, author, professor, and beloved pastor, Henri Nouwen (now deceased) who wrote thirty-nine books on the spiritual life.

Care is something other than cure. Cure means "change." A doctor, a lawyer, a minister, a social worker—they all want to use their professional skills to bring about changes in other people's lives. They get paid for whatever kind of cure they can bring about. But cure, desirable as it may be, can easily become violent, manipulative, and even destructive if it does not grow out of care. Care is being with, crying out with, suffering with, feeling with. Care is compassion. It is claiming the truth that the other person is my brother or sister, human, mortal, vulnerable, like I am.

When care is our first concern, cure can be received as a gift. Often, we are not able to cure, but we are always able to care. To care is to be human.[2]

Looking back on Mike's intervention, two qualities are most apparent to me. First, Mike's care for me exceeded any concern he might have had about how I would respond. Second, his love was unconditional. Beyond any reasonable doubt, his priority was not to fix me but to care for me.

Just as Mike did for me, we too have opportunities to assist other people in seeing their blind spots. Some of these people are average, middle-of-the-road folks like me. Others live on the rough and raw fringes of society. Others are living the "good life" on "easy street." Regardless of our status and reputation, we all have blind spots. They're often unsightly, threatening, and dangerous. Sometimes they're enormous, menacing, and baffling. Some blind spots don't appear very often, remaining carefully camouflaged in hidden places. Some days, our blind spots are large and in charge. Yet the blind spots we're most inclined to see are not our own but belong to another.

Be Encouraged

Truth often becomes a blind spot when it's something we don't wish to hear or say to another person or to God. But Jesus teaches that it's better to hear or tell hurtful truths than comforting lies and he goes the second mile by showing us the way.

Jesus also makes a remarkable promise to those who dare to follow him. He says, "You are truly my disciples if you remain faithful to my teachings. And you will know the truth, and the truth will set you free" (John 8:31–32). This reality is an extraordinary challenge and an exhilarating promise. The challenge, "to remain faithful to my teachings," isn't oppressive or especially difficult; it's extremely gracious. It is an invitation to live in a wonderful home with no great price attached *to it*. However, it does have magnificent benefits promised *from it*.

Get Engaged

Here's a question I hope you will sincerely and truthfully ponder:

- What do your current habits and practices say about how you're responding to Jesus's *extraordinary challenge* and *exhilarating promise*? Do you detect or wonder about having any blind spots?
- Are you willing to ask those who know you best and observe how you live (publicly and privately); whether you appear to be "remaining faithful to Jesus's teachings"? If so, please do. If you are not willing to ask, why?

CHAPTER 7

How Do I Break Free
of Blind Spots?

If you always do what you've always done, you'll
always get what you've always got. — Henry Ford

(Tim)

Stuck

Phil Connors was stuck. He was a weatherman for
a local news station in Pittsburgh, Pennsylvania. His
management ignored his talents. Trivial news assign-
ments added to his frustration. The final straw came
when Phil and his producer, Rita, were assigned to cover
the annual Groundhog Day festivities in Punxsutawney,
Pennsylvania.

On February 2nd, everyone in the town gath-
ers to celebrate the appearance of a groundhog named
Punxsutawney Phil. What happens when he emerges from
his home in the ground is said to predict the weather for
the next six weeks. If he sees his shadow, there will be
six more weeks of winter weather. If he doesn't see his

shadow, the town can look forward to an early spring. The actual celebration dates back to 1887, but Punxsutawney Phil became an international celebrity thanks to the 1993 comedy film, *Groundhog Day*, starring Bill Murray as the weatherman.

In addition to being stuck, Murray's character Phil Connors is rude, obnoxious, and arrogant. He doesn't hide his contempt for this assignment. In his opinion, it is a waste of time. Phil planned to get in and get out, the sooner, the better.

Phil, Rita, and their cameraman, Larry, arrive February 1 to prepare for the news story. The next morning Phil wakes precisely at 6 a.m. to the sound of Sonny and Cher's song, "I Got You Babe" on the radio. There were lots of festivities for the day. Rita wants to stay, but Phil is not interested. He plans to do a quick report on Punxsutawney Phil and head back to Pittsburgh. He hopes this silly groundhog will quickly appear so he can consider this assignment complete.

But a blizzard sets in and Phil, Rita, and Larry are stranded in Punxsutawney. The locals enjoy the festivities despite the weather, but Phil has no interest in joining the party. He heads to bed early, hoping the storm clears so they can at least get home the next day. Unfortunately for Phil, that's when the time loop begins.

The next morning at precisely 6 a.m., the same song, "I Got You Babe," plays on the radio. Phil eventually realizes that he is reliving the previous day all over again. At one point he is so discouraged he says, "Well, what if there was no tomorrow? There wasn't one today."

The day repeats itself over and over. Phil wakes each morning at 6 a.m. to the same song and the same miserable routine. At first, Phil decides to have some fun. Since there don't appear to be any consequences for his actions, why not live a little? He spends the first few days binge drinking, engaging in one-night stands, and driving recklessly. However that "fun" spirals down to a feeling of discouragement and despair. But each morning, he wakes at 6 a.m. to the same familiar tune and starts the day all over again. There's a revealing scene in the movie where Phil is sitting at a bowling alley with a couple of the town drunks. He asks, "What would you do if you were stuck in one place and every day was exactly the same and nothing that you did mattered?" One of the drunks sadly replies, "That about sums it up for me."

Time to Break the Loop

Have you ever felt like that sums it up for you as well? Do you ever find your day filled with meaningless stuff? Do you feel trapped or stagnant? Do you seem to be living the same day over and over? Perhaps you are trapped in days of monotony only to hear the alarm sound at 6 a.m. to the same familiar tune.

Blind spots can be the reason why we feel stuck. We are often more comfortable living in the past than we are breaking free and facing the future. The past is familiar and the future is unknown. Our blind spots can produce a fear of facing the unknown, especially when we are uncertain about who we might become.

Although identifying a blind spot is a significant step in the right direction, it's only half the battle. Removing it requires a plan of attack. Maybe you have identified a blind spot but you can't seem to break out to remove it.

Have you ever wanted to make a change in your life but something is holding you back? Perhaps you've done the hard work of exposing a blind spot, but you don't know how to get rid of it. Maybe it's a behavior that you've tried to change. Maybe it's something with your health, job, marriage, relationships, financial situation, or even your spiritual life. Even the list can be exhausting! Trying to get unstuck is one of the most popular topics in our society today. Self-help books are filled with plans of attack. A Google search will produce pages and pages of websites offering help. And then there is our hopeful fascination with New Year's resolutions!

A friend of mine from Australia said, "Life doesn't change, mate, unless you shift gears now and then." And I love the words of Henry Ford: "If you always do what you've always done, you'll always get what you've always got."

Just Do Something

An initial impulse for breaking free is to DO something. That was Phil Connors's plan of attack. He tried all kinds of different "stuff" to see if he could break out of his time loop. But it wasn't until his heart changed that he finally woke up to a brand-new day.

I tend to think strategically, so I quickly map out a new list of things to do to get me out of a rut. Countless times I've sat down on Sunday night and said, "This week is going to be different." I'm determined to find that magical formula that will help me shift gears.

The problem with starting at the "doing stage" is that it never seems to work. Sure, it can make a difference for a day or two. You might even see temporary change for a couple of weeks or months. But statistics show that it usually won't last, and we find ourselves back at the starting blocks.

Let me clarify. Disciplines that you implement in your life to help you break free and experience change are beneficial. I love structure and have many disciplines that guide my life. However, in my experience, if you jump to the plan without seeing the real reason for the problem, it usually doesn't last. I suggest backing up to obtain a clear vision as a first step.

Clarity

First, you have to identify what being "unstuck" looks like. If you are standing at "A" and your goal is to reach "B," your first task at hand is to clearly identify what "B" looks like. How will your life be transformed when you arrive at "B"? The vision has to be clear, so you know where to begin. The vision also has to be clear, so you don't get distracted in your search for "B."

One of the biggest mistakes we make in response to our desire to change is our failure to define the outcome. We start an exercise routine on January 1, but have we taken the time to envision what our bodies might look and feel like six months later? How will our new physical health affect our lives? Without that vision in mind, we will probably run out of gas as soon as we face the first obstacle that stands in our way. The priority of reaching our "B" can easily lose its significance when distractions fill our day. Soon we lose sight of "B" and our quest eventually ends with fewer and fewer trips to the gym each week.

Recently I interviewed a friend for my podcast, *Discover Blindspots*. Simon was a great cyclist in South Africa as a young athlete. He won all the top races in his country and was on track for a successful pro career. Then, in his early twenties, he found himself in a hotel room in a foreign country, recovering after surgery for an unexpected leg injury while on tour. He had two options. He could choose self-pity and give up on his dreams or he could choose to use those weeks of recovery to write out his life plan. Simon chose the second option and tried to capture a vision of what his full recovery could look like. He wanted to clearly define his "B." He wanted to break free. In the months that followed, he fully recovered, to the surprise of many, and went on to a successful career. So many times when tragedy strikes, we lose our vision. It becomes hard to look ahead because of the obstacles staring us in the face. We have to find something that can change our perspective and bring our blind spot obstacles into view. It's like climbing a tall tree to get a better view.

Tree Climbing

Most kids love to climb a tree, but to hang out in a tree house is even better. I didn't have a tree house when I was a kid, but when I started my own company, we had several large pieces of machinery on the property with a platform at the top. I loved climbing up to that platform on a Sunday afternoon when no one was around. I would quietly look out over the plant. That spot was a great place to plan the next steps for the company. It was one of the few times that I felt the clock stop for a few minutes so I could check the pulse of my future. I had many long conversations with God while on top of that platform.

Maybe because of that, I love the biblical story about a guy who decided to do some climbing, who probably never dreamed it would alter the course of his life. He simply wanted to see this famous man that people were claiming was the Messiah! Since he was a small man, he had to be creative to obtain a better view. What he didn't realize was the object of his new perspective would change his life!

Wee Little Man

The story is about a "wee little man" named Zacchaeus. He was a tax collector, which was not the most popular career choice in first-century Israel. Collecting money for the Roman government would not make you a crowd favorite.

Zacchaeus was stuck. Each morning he woke to the same familiar tune of extorting money from the Jewish people. If they owed $1,000 in taxes, he might charge $1,500 so he could keep the extra $500. If people refused to pay, he would notify his collection agency and Herod's soldiers would appear.

Although we don't know a lot about Zacchaeus, his desire to get a glimpse of Jesus tells us that he was searching for something more than what he had. Although he may have been wealthy financially, spiritually he was bankrupt.

> He tried to get a look at Jesus, but he was too short to see over the crowd. So he ran ahead and climbed a sycamore-fig tree beside the road, for Jesus was going to pass that way. (Luke 19:3–4)

I love Zacchaeus's quick thinking. It may have been one of his tax collecting skills. A good revenue agent has to be quick on his feet! Zacchaeus wanted to see the man who was causing such a stir in his community. At this point in Jesus's ministry, his reputation usually brought large crowds that anxiously awaited his arrival to a new town. Zacchaeus was determined not to be left out so he shimmied up a tree. Sycamore trees could reach forty feet tall, which would provide a great view. Little did Zacchaeus know what would happen once he got a clear view of Jesus.

Once Your Perspective Changes

Our perspective is oftentimes clouded by blind spots. Several years ago I went to the eye doctor for a normal checkup. An expression of growing concern became apparent as he continued to shine lights into the corners of my eyes. Finally he informed me that I had a cataract in one of my eyes. He claimed that it was clouding my vision yet I had no idea there was a problem. Several weeks later the cataract was surgically removed. The following morning I thought my wife had changed the lighting in our home. All of a sudden everything was so bright and clear!

Habit #2 of Steven Covey's *Seven Habits of Highly Successful Living* is "Begin with the end in mind." When the vision is clear, the options become fewer, and the decisions easier. As a leader, I've had to make many decisions. Some were good, others not so much. The most successful decisions were ones where I sought clarity first. Before you can get unstuck and remove a dangerous blind spot in your life, you have to see the dysfunction it has caused and the freedom it can bring once it's removed.

A New Perspective

Change for the sake of change can be an enticing blind spot within itself. I can't count the number of people I've talked to that decided a change of scenery would solve their problems. In my years of hiring new staff, one of the first things I look for in a résumé is how often someone changed jobs. Many times it is a sign of a blind spot they are not facing. Perhaps they have believed that a new career or a change of scenery will suddenly remove past dysfunctions. Instead of breaking out of our blind spots, we choose to run from them, but they follow us to our new location.

In *Ground Hog Day*, Phil Connors searched for a new perspective in order to break free. His binge drinking, one-night stands, and reckless driving certainly provided for what might appear to be an exciting today, but tomorrow he would wake up to the same familiar song.

Zacchaeus was searching for a new perspective as well. Little did he know that an encounter with Jesus would provide a new perspective that would dramatically change his life. Although a change of scenery for clarity can be helpful, the focal point of your new perspective is essential.

> When Jesus came by, he looked up at Zacchaeus and called him by name. "Zacchaeus!" he said. "Quick, come down! I must be a guest in your home today."
> (Luke 19:5)

What I love about this interaction is that Jesus engaged Zacchaeus right where he was. Often we feel that it's on us to search for and find Jesus. Or we might think that we have to remove our own sinful blind spots before we can come to Jesus. Change feels like it is all on us. But Zacchaeus just climbs a tree and Jesus finds him. Jesus breaks into Zacchaeus's world and invites himself for dinner.

Jesus is also knocking on the door of your heart, asking for you to swing wide the door and invite him in. He says, "Look! I stand at the door and knock. If you hear my voice and open the door, I will come in, and we will share a meal together as friends" (Revelation 3:20). And that's exactly what Jesus did! He still does. He is waiting to be the object of our new perspective. He is willing to meet us right where we are, blind spots and all.

Zacchaeus heeded the call of Jesus:

> Zacchaeus quickly climbed down and took Jesus to his house in great excitement and joy. (Luke 19:6)

Scripture doesn't allow us to hear the conversation between Jesus and Zacchaeus. I have often wondered why. I've come to the conclusion that perhaps it was because it was a holy moment, just like breaking free from the chains in our lives. Whatever the discussion, Zacchaeus is now ready to take action and begin a life free of sinful blind spots!

Taking Action

Now it's time to do something! It's time for Zacchaeus to take a new step. A step away from his past and toward a new and brighter future. Because when you meet Jesus, everything changes. Seeing Jesus for who he is—your brother, friend, Savior, and Lord—brings clarity about your own life. As you see Jesus, you see yourself and his love gives you the power to turn from your sins—both the ones you are blind to and the ones you know about. That's exactly what happened to Zacchaeus. Before he met Jesus it was business as usual, but now everything has changed. Christ is the center of his new life and that meant new steps of faith.

> Meanwhile, Zacchaeus stood before the Lord and said, "I will give half my wealth to the poor, Lord, and if I have cheated people on their taxes, I will give them back four times as much!" (Luke 19:8)

Zacchaeus is ready to let go of his old life of deceit and corruption. Zacchaeus needed to let go of the idol he worshiped—money. Like him, before we can move forward and begin a new life, we have to be willing to let go of the past. In order to reach our "B," we have to be willing to leave our current "A." For a tax collector to return money he had extorted was evidence that Zacchaeus had truly seen the Savior. This was not a minor adjustment but a complete renovation of his heart. Turning toward Jesus means also turning away from sin and asking and accepting forgiveness from him.

Jesus affirms Zacchaeus's courageous step:

> Jesus responded, "Salvation has come to this home today, for this man has shown himself to be a true son of Abraham." (Luke 19:9)

Going back to *Groundhog Day*, our weatherman Phil breaks free also. He spends his final Groundhog Day caring for others, and at 6 a.m. the next morning he wakes up to a new song and a brand-new day. Phil's change of heart makes for a great story, but the heart change of turning toward Jesus brings something deeper and truer to our lives—"salvation comes to our house" when we look to Jesus. In the light of his love we can see our sinful blind spots and know we are forgiven. His love gives us the courage to ask for and receive forgiveness. And that becomes the new rhythm of our lives.

Be Encouraged

So where are you? What in your life do you need to address? Are there things in your life that you need to walk away from? Are there blind spots that are keeping you at "A" when you long to take a step toward your new "B"? Take a moment right now and ask the Spirit to show you what he wants to do in your life. Remember, the Holy Spirit can guide your path. The Spirit can provide the clarity, conviction, and courage to permanently move forward. And soon you may hear Jesus say, "Change has come upon this house today!"

Get Engaged

Think of something in your life that you would like to change. First, write down what change would actually look like. Be as descriptive as you can. Next, write down all the obstacles that have stood in your way in the past. Make sure Jesus is at the center of your new perspective.

Recently I had lunch with a friend. We hadn't seen each other in a while but our last interaction left our relationship feeling fractured. At the end of the lunch, he apologized for anything he had done to create the tension. Ironically I confessed that I had scheduled the lunch to confess a blind spot that had affected my behavior. I told him my wrong response to him was a burden I had been carrying around since our last interaction and that God had pressed on me to seek restoration. I knew that I needed to ask God and my friend for forgiveness. He graciously forgave me and we both left with a renewed sense of joy in our relationship. Acknowledging my blind spot and asking for forgiveness meant that there wasn't anything still hindering my relationship with the Lord or with my friend.

Ask God to show you what blind spot might be holding you back. Are there attitudes and desires that you need to turn from? Zacchaeus turned from greed when he met Jesus. What might the Spirit be impressing on your heart as something you need to turn from? Ask Jesus to forgive you for those things that come to your mind. Remember that he came to "seek and save the lost." It's OK to admit you are lost without Jesus—going your own way, trying to do life on your terms. Telling Jesus the truth about yourself will bring freedom and joy. He died so that you could be free to love him and love others.

Finally, jot down your first courageous step. Be aware that the first step is usually the hardest. I fought for the longest time before scheduling the lunch with my friend. Face your fears of rejection and failure, and trust in Jesus to walk with you through the journey. Soon you will wake up to a new song and a new day.

CHAPTER 8

How Do I Prevent My Blind Spots from Returning?

I like your Christ; I do not like your Christians. Your Christians are so unlike your Christ. — Mahatma Gandhi

(Tim)

The Phone Call

It was a beautiful Saturday morning in early June. I was out for my usual Saturday bike ride with some of my cycling buddies. We were riding a familiar route and had stopped at our regular place to regroup.

My phone rang, and by the time I dug it out of my back pocket, I had missed the call. I noticed it was from an unknown number, so I assumed it was a sales call or the wrong number. A few minutes later my phone rang again. This time it was my wife, Stacy. When I answered, I heard these words: "Tim, Fletcher was in an accident this morning on the way home from the beach. He's OK. He had two friends in the car with him, and they are OK as well. It sounds like the car was totaled. He's about two hours from home. He just tried to call you from someone's phone who stopped to help on the side of the road. We need to figure out a plan."

My heart stopped for a minute, but I rested on the words, "He's OK." I told my cycling friends what happened and that I was going to head back home. It would take me about forty-five minutes to get there. As I pedaled home, my mind started racing. I had all kinds of questions. What happened? Was he speeding? Did he accidentally run off the road? Did another car hit him? Did he fall asleep at the wheel? Was he distracted?

By the time I got home, Stacy had informed me that one of the other parents were on their way to pick the kids up. I quickly called the unknown number of the missed call because I wanted to hear Fletcher's voice. A woman answered and handed him the phone. Immediately I could tell he was shaken. He couldn't talk long because the Highway Patrol and EMTs were there and needed his attention. I told him to call me back as soon as he could. With my mind still racing, I launched into a plan of attack with insurance and logistics. I needed to stay busy while waiting for more information from Fletcher.

Soon the phone rang. It was Fletcher. He proceeded to tell me more of the details. He and two of his friends had left early to head back home. He had to work that day, so he wanted to be back in plenty of time. He was driving on a section of road with little traffic. The speed limit was 55 mph and he had his cruise control set. He had just passed a car and was still in the passing lane when suddenly his car violently jerked to the left off the road. He tried to adjust but lost control of the vehicle. The next thing he remembered was the car turning over. It flipped twice and landed back on its wheels. At that point, he noticed fire outside his driver's side window. He yelled to his buddies to get out of the car. As they exited and ran away to a safe distance, they watched the vehicle go up in flames within a few minutes. They were all in shock.

Shortly afterward, the highway patrol officer called to inform me that Fletcher and his friends would be taken to the patrol station in that area until a parent could pick them up. He added, "Sir, I've seen a lot of accidents in my day. Ninety-nine percent of the time nobody would have survived. Your son and his friends were very fortunate."

A few hours later, the wrecker service called. The man called to ask if I could provide the tag number to the car. I asked, "Aren't you looking at the car? Can't you tell?" He said, "Sir, I don't think you understand. This car is burned so badly you can't read the license plate. Somebody was looking out for your son."

To this day we still don't know what happened. It could have been a pothole, a blown tire, or a malfunction with the steering of the car. We do know that something unseen almost took my son's life. I would have done anything to prevent it from happening. I think most parents would do anything to keep their child from danger, especially when it's something they can't anticipate or see.

Prevention

Prevention is often forgotten in today's world. We seem more interested in fixing the problem after the fact than taking steps to prevent it before it happens. It's a hospital at the bottom of the cliff as opposed to a guardrail at the top. The insurance industry is designed to help people put their lives back together after a catastrophe. I wish the insurance we purchase could prevent the accidents from happening!

105

I wish the same was possible with blind spots. Sure, sometimes we honestly can't see a blind spot until it's too late. Our only option is to focus on removing it as opposed to preventing it. Blind spots love to find secret hiding places in our lives and, at an opportune moment, rear their ugly heads. Is there a way to prevent them from developing? What about a plan to stop those that try to return after we've worked hard to get rid of them?

Spiritual Insurance

On April 29, 1972, I discovered the ultimate prevention insurance to eliminate bad things in my life, or so I thought. I was twelve years old and fortunate to have two loving parents of great faith. They both were deeply involved in our church. Both of my parents passed away in my early thirties. I am eternally grateful for the spiritual foundation they provided in my first thirty years.

On that night in April, I decided to say yes to Jesus. Boy, I was relieved! Before that time, the idea of finding spiritual insurance to get into heaven consumed me. I saw it as similar to passing a class at school. As long as I completed all the homework and made good grades on all the tests, I would move to the next level. But I struggled to know the passing grade for heaven. The harder I tried, the more difficult it was to keep sin—and my blind spots about them—away. Could they cause me to fail the class? That night, I was overjoyed because I thought I had conquered all my temptations and struggles. I thought God would wrap me in a bubble and protect me the rest of my life. I expected smooth sailing from that point forward. Obviously, my theological understanding of salvation needed refining.

That protected feeling only lasted for a couple of days. Soon I found myself falling back into my old habits.

I didn't understand. Wasn't the hard part over? Wasn't this part of the journey supposed to be downhill with the wind at my back?

My initial plan of attack after a few Sundays was to respond to the altar call at the end of the church service. At our small church, periodically the pastor would make the altar available for those who wanted to ask for forgiveness and give their life to Jesus. So I decided to accept the offer, again! Perhaps this could provide additional insurance if I missed something the first time.

Afterward, I thought I noticed strange looks from the congregation. They probably thought, "Didn't he just say yes to Jesus a few weeks ago?" But it seemed to help, and I felt renewed again. I was ready to take on the world and fight off the bad guys. That is, until a few days later when I felt the same sinful urges. So I decided to try the altar again a few weeks later. I was determined to regain my "sin fighting" confidence. That pattern continued over the next couple of months until my parents finally pulled me aside and explained the fine print of my new spiritual insurance. In essence, trying to be good enough was not going to work!

Recently I had lunch with a friend, and we were discussing the concept of blind spots. He said, "Tim, why do Christ followers seem to struggle with blind spots more than anyone else?" As I've reflected on the question, I suspect it's because of a false expectation we place on God. We easily fall into the trap of thinking that once we punch our salvation ticket, the hard work is over. Dangerous, sinful blind spots don't stand a chance anymore. But that theological myth has been shattered over the years through stories of devout Christian leaders derailed by their sins and the blind spots that developed around them. These blind spots for a time hid moral failures, financial demons, addiction nightmares, and deadly egos that were meanwhile wreaking havoc in their lives. But eventually they were exposed. I love the famous quote from Mahatma Gandhi:

"I like your Christ; I do not like your Christians. Your Christians are so unlike your Christ."

Jesus Plus Nothing

In Paul's letter to the Galatians, he warned the church against the trap I fell into as a young believer. Some of the new, non-Jewish believers were being told to obey the traditional Jewish rules and laws in addition to following Jesus.

The original purpose of the law was to help identify sins that would separate people from God and would require a sacrifice to atone for the sin. It was given to help God's people understand God's holiness and their need for forgiveness when they did not meet that standard— which God knew they could never do on their own. But over time, some people saw the law as something they *could* keep if they tried hard enough. At the time, 613 laws consisted of 365 things you couldn't do and 248 things you had to do each day. Law-keeping became a competition to measure one person's performance against another's. The better your score, the higher you ranked. The spotlight moved from growing closer to God, with a humble reliance on his forgiveness and mercy, to how many rules you kept each day.

Paul, on the other hand, preached "Jesus plus nothing." In other words, you didn't need to add a list of rules to keep to qualify for salvation. Paul's primary purpose was to uphold the unique saving power of the cross. If salvation requires adding things to Christ's death on the cross for our sins, then it minimizes the significance of

Jesus's death and resurrection. Jesus kept the law perfectly in the way we could not, so when he died for *our* sins, it meant we were no longer obligated to keep the law ourselves. The law provides moral guidelines for our lives, but it cannot save us.

> "Don't misunderstand why I have come. I did not come to abolish the law of Moses or the writings of the prophets. No, I came to accomplish their purpose." (Matthew 5:17)

The Guide

In Galatians 5 Paul reminds us of the Guide who walks with us once we decide to follow Jesus.

> So I say, let the Holy Spirit guide your lives. Then you won't be doing what your sinful nature craves. (Galatians 5:16)

When you say yes to Jesus, the Holy Spirit takes up residence inside you. For many, that's a strange thought. In fact, often the Holy Spirit is overlooked because we don't understand. To simplify, it's God's Spirit living within you to provide a compass for your life. The Spirit comforts, guides, and reminds you of the truth. The Spirit can give you the right words to say and the spiritual power to do good things and to follow Jesus. The entrance of the Holy Spirit into your heart marks the starting point of the Christian life. We do not belong to Christ if we do not have the Spirit. The Holy Spirit guides and empowers us to become more like Christ. As he does, he reveals our sins and blind spots. He helps us to turn away from them and seek God's forgiveness. He provides the spiritual strength we need to overcome them and keep them from regaining their hold on us. God asks us to turn our blind spots over to the Spirit to be purged and to guard our hearts if they decide to return. That sounds like great prevention insurance, doesn't it?

The Tension

Still, Paul wants us to be aware of the tension we encounter every day.

> The sinful nature wants to do evil, which is just the opposite of what the Spirit wants. And the Spirit gives us desires that are the opposite of what the sinful nature desires. These two forces are constantly fighting each other, so you are not free to carry out your good intentions. (Galatians 5:17)

I felt that tension immediately after I said yes to Jesus and I feel that same tension today. This tension has derailed many Christ followers when dangerous blind spots reenter their lives. We underestimate the sinful nature that still resides inside us. We underestimate the battle that takes place each day. Though we have a new life in Christ, we also have a mind and body that are still enticed by our sinful desires. Whenever we set out to follow the leading of the Holy Spirit, we can expect our sinful flesh to rise up in opposition.

Two Operating Systems

Next, Paul lays out two specific lists. The first lists the sins and dysfunction that are the breeding ground for blind spots.

When you follow the desires of your sinful nature, the results are very clear: sexual immorality, impurity, lustful pleasures, idolatry, sorcery, hostility, quarreling, jealousy, outbursts of anger, selfish ambition, dissension, division, envy, drunkenness, wild parties, and other sins like these. Let me tell you again, as I have before, that anyone living that sort of life will not inherit the Kingdom of God. (Galatians 5:19–21)

Think about it this way. We have two operating systems that can run our lives. One is the flesh operating system (our natural, fallen human nature), and the other is the Holy Spirit operating system.

I remember when I made the switch from a PC to a Mac. At first, I was afraid to let go of my PC programs, so I used software that allowed me to switch back and forth. Eventually, it was too frustrating, so I finally eliminated the PC from my life.

Paul's first list reminds us of the dangers of allowing the flesh operating system to take control. When I first said yes to Jesus at age twelve, I thought I had automatically removed the flesh operating system, just as I later removed Windows from my Mac computer. But the reality is that we deal with the temptations of the flesh operating system for the rest of our lives. And that operating system encourages sin, and the blind spots that hide them, to flourish.

Prevention Insurance

Paul's next list describes what the Holy Spirit grows in our heart in place of these blind spots. I see them as the best kind of prevention insurance.

But the Holy Spirit produces this kind of fruit in our lives: love, joy, peace, patience, kindness, goodness, faithfulness, gentleness, and self-control. (Galatians 5:22–23)

When the Holy Spirit operating system is in control, these fruits will grow and post a "no vacancy" sign on your heart for the sins and blind spots in your life. There is little room for a blind spot to live in a heart filled with these nine fruits. They are evidence of a changed life and a heart seeking to be blind spot free!

Nailed to the Cross

Finally, Paul reinforces the challenge we face.

Those who belong to Christ Jesus have nailed the passions and desires of their sinful nature to his cross and crucified them there. (Galatians 5:24)

The process takes time. I thought my sinful passions and desires were nailed to the cross on that April evening. And as far as my standing and acceptance with God is concerned, they were. I was completely forgiven and cleansed of my sins when I trusted Jesus as my Savior and gave my life to him. I became God's child and the Holy Spirit came to live within me.

But that heavenly reality is experienced differently on earth, where my fallen human nature coexists with the Holy Spirit within me. I still have to battle sin and blind spots, and in that sense I have to nail a few more sins and desire to the cross as the Holy Spirit helps me to see them. Crucifixion was a brutal, painful death because it was slow. It could take a few hours to a few days for the person to finally die. Similarly, our sinful nature, although it has been nailed to the cross, can take time to die. And we might find that our flesh operating system has to be re-crucified daily. We will always face the possibility of sin and its deadly blind spots reentering our lives. But we now have a choice and we can enlist the help of the Spirit to fight the battle each day.

Mirrors

So what's the plan? I would love to think that I could wake up each morning and allow my Holy Spirit operating system to have full control of my life. I would also love to think that I would eat right, exercise, and spend my money wisely each day without being tempted to stray in the opposite direction. In reality, we need a plan to keep us on track.

While writing this book, I have read a lot about the problem of blind spots while driving. Almost every article talks about the significance of mirrors and their adjustments. The rearview mirror should be set to give you the best view from behind. The side mirrors should be adjusted to ensure that you have a clear view on your left and right. It's also important to note that my mirror settings are not the same as my wife's. When I drive Stacy's car, I have to adjust the mirrors so that I can see. She has to readjust them when she gets the car back. We would never think of driving without making those adjustments. But so many times in life we begin our day and never adjust our spiritual mirrors.

These mirrors help you to look inside in ways that are essential. These mirrors may be the spiritual disciplines or practices you follow each day. Let me leave you with three mirrors that have been helpful in my life. There are others I have used throughout the years, but these three have been most helpful to me in battling sin and keeping dangerous blind spots from returning. They also help me monitor the growth of the fruit of the Spirit in my life.

Read

There are many good books that I want to read, but there is one that I have found important to consume every day. That book is God's Word. Throughout my life, I have read the Bible piece by piece. Sometimes I read a verse a day or maybe a chapter or two. When I was young, I even tried the old "finger trick"—the one where I opened the book and pointed to a passage of Scripture, hoping it would solve my current problem.

Several years ago, I heard a pastor mention that reading through the Bible in a year only takes fifteen minutes a day. I didn't believe it, so I tested his statement and, for the past five years, I have read the Bible cover to cover each year. It only took fifteen minutes a day! There are many Scripture reading plans. You can read it on your phone, your tablet, and even listen in your car. Whatever way you do it, I encourage you to add the "mirror" of reading Scripture to your life. The Holy Spirit can speak through the words you read and help you determine which operating system will control your life.

One-on-One

The ultimate mirror in our life is our heavenly Father. Through his guidance, grace, and mercy, he will shape our lives. However, for that to happen, we have to spend time with him. Carving out daily time with your heavenly Father is vital. But remember, this takes different forms. It's not just you talking TO God. Sometimes your time with him will consist of simply sitting WITH God. Perhaps he has something he wants to say to you through the Holy Spirit. Often, when my one-on-one time only consists of talking TO God, I've wondered if God ever wanted to say, "I had a lot to say to you, but you never gave me a chance to speak." My best ideas in life have always come from listening. Make sure you give God a chance to speak to you. Maybe it's just a minute or two sitting in silence. Perhaps you are frustrated because you haven't heard anything. But remember, God speaks in mysterious ways. What he says to you today may not be heard for weeks or months down the road. So don't forget to give God his time.

People

A final, critical spiritual mirror is people in our lives who can see what we can't see. As Fil and I have been writing this book, we have declared each other blind spot partners. Numerous times I have walked in Fil's office and asked, "Is this a blind spot I'm missing?" My wife, Stacy, has been my blind spot partner for thirty-three years. My four kids must have X-ray vision because they are quick to point out my blind spots.

But before this can happen, you have to be open and receptive to input. Over my life, I have had a few friends who struggled with feedback. They resisted looking into these mirrors to face their dreaded blind spots. The work is hard, but the freedom that comes is worth the hard work.

One Final Thing: Reminders

I love taking Communion. I love how Jesus modeled the Lord's Supper to remind us of his incredible grace and mercy. I need reminders in my life to help me choose the Holy Spirit operating system each day.

On my right wrist, I wear a bracelet that connects to one half of a dime. When my son, Fletcher, came home from his car accident, he removed his shoe to find a single dime. Other than the clothes on his back, this dime was the only thing that made it out of the car. For Father's Day that year, he had it cut in half. He wears the other half on his left wrist. It's a reminder of God's grace for his life that day. It's also a reminder of the unseen dangers that can cause a car to crash and life to derail. I guess you could consider it one of our mirrors.

Be Encouraged

Identifying sin and removing blind spots is hard work. Keeping your mirrors adjusted so they don't reappear is even harder. The good news is that we don't have to do it alone. As the Holy Spirit guides your path, he will help you see what you need to see.

Make sure your mirrors are in place to give you the best view of the life God has intended for you. As they say, an ounce of prevention is worth a pound of cure. Choose to allow your Holy Spirit operating system to manage your daily life by relying on your mirrors, and the spiritual fruit that results will help prevent the sinful blind spots from returning.

Get Engaged

Identify a few mirrors in your life. I have outlined three that have proven faithful to me. Spend some time determining the right mirrors for you. Then carve out time in your schedule to use these mirrors daily. Be intentional about your plan and you will soon notice that your Holy Spirit operating system is at work to help keep dangerous blind spots from returning to your life.

CHAPTER 9

Eliminating Blind Spots

The longing for something more, no matter how weak or crackling with heat, is evidence that God is already at work in your life. — Adele Calhoun, *Spiritual Disciplines Handbook*

(Fil)

Call it "bravery" or "ignorance on fire," no matter what it was that possessed me, I recently asked my wife to identify one of my blind spots. You can probably guess the outcome but humor me for a moment. To her credit, she did her best to change the subject and wiggle out of answering. But my persistence finally provoked her response. As gently as she could, she claimed that, depending on the issue, I tend to become defensive when receiving feedback.

And my response? "I don't know what you mean. That's not how I see it."

And her reply? "Precisely. That's why it's called a blind spot."

The next thirty minutes were spent in an intense debate as I became increasingly defensive about being defensive when receiving a critique.

Our Heart's Desires

The conversation with my wife offers proof that we can know what our blind spots are if we care to—or more accurately if we *dare* to. But I'll give this word of caution: be sure that you sincerely want to know. Having your sins and blind spots exposed can be shocking, humiliating, painful, and disappointing. It helps to have a tough hide and a tender heart. A direct seek-and-destroy attack on your blind spots, whether they're the result of innocent ignorance or blatant denial, is not child's play. Denial is far trickier than mere ignorance. It isn't the failure to process information. Instead, it's the capacity for handling information while routinely refusing to allow it entry into our consciousness.

Our minds don't accomplish this feat without reason or practice. This phenomenon occurs only when the news we have become blind to is so disturbing, frightening, or threatening that accepting it would extinguish our view of ourselves or the world. On the other hand, continual, courageous, honest, and sincere movement—no matter how gradual—toward seeing the entire truth about our life—the good, the bad, the ugly, and the beautiful—is the path to eliminating our blind spots. It's the only reliable foundation for enduring relationships, fruitful endeavors, and lasting peace. Hunting down and exposing our blind spots (or allowing them to be detected) is a daring and risky adventure, but it's worth the cost.

Our deepest desires give shape and direction to our spiritual journey. The people who make gradual yet steady progress toward living with fewer blind spots are driven by a desire that inhabits their souls while they remain open to the Spirit of God and those around them for assistance. More often than we imagine, we get what we most desire. Therefore, it's crucial for our lives to be grounded in God and that we allow God to purge and purify our desires. Don't be misled or mistaken: following Jesus isn't about the elimination of desire. It's about the refinement and refocusing of our desire. Our desires influence the daily outcome of our lives. "Life is shaped by the end you live for," wrote Thomas Merton. "You are made in the image of what you desire."[1] Nothing will propel you forward in your quest to live blind spot free more than nurturing that desire.

Genuine and Complete

One of my Bible heroes is Nathanael. We rarely hear of him, but he was singled out by Jesus, who commented on a specific aspect of his character. Nathanael had fewer blind spots than most people Jesus encountered. "The next day Jesus decided to go to Galilee. He found Philip and said to him, 'Come, follow me.' . . . Philip went to look for Nathanael and told him, 'We have found the very person Moses and the prophets wrote about! His name is Jesus, the son of Joseph from Nazareth.' 'Nazareth!' exclaimed Nathanael. 'Can anything good come from Nazareth?' 'Come and see for yourself,' Philip replied. As they approached, Jesus said, 'Now here is a genuine son of Israel—a man of complete integrity'" (John 1:43, 45–47).

Jesus considered "complete integrity" to be remarkable, presumably because it is so rare. In saying that Nathaniel was "genuine . . . a man of complete integrity," Jesus meant that he was entirely without pretense or hypocrisy. Nathanael was the type of man who meant what he said and said what he meant. He didn't have hidden agendas or ulterior motives. If he wanted something, he would openly and honestly say what he wanted and why. He would not trick or manipulate people. Neither would he use anybody.

Above all, being a man of "complete integrity" means that we are ruthlessly honest *with ourselves* and *about ourselves*. When a person with this quality reads about specific faults in the Bible, they readily accept that those faults are to be found in them. They don't assume that they're without those flaws and that they are only to be found in others.

People with "complete integrity" are sincere and genuine and have a quality of innocence about them. They are tender rather than hardened, and the truth matters to them. This kind of person is referred to in Psalm 32:2: "What joy for those whose record the LORD has cleared of guilt, whose lives are lived in complete honesty!"

Jesus's knowledge of Nathanael is miraculous. Jesus knows people's identities deep down inside, and he wants them to know who they are or are going to be as well, and to know what he thinks of them.

Transformational Knowing

A book that has inspired and guided my pilgrimage toward living with fewer blind spots is *The Gift of Being Yourself* by David Benner. With Christlike compassion and Spirit-infused insight, Benner demonstrates that the two great tasks of life—knowing God and knowing ourselves—converge into a single and spectacular adventure drawing us into the open, waiting arms of our loving God.

"Christian spirituality involves a transformation of the self," Benner writes "that occurs only when God and self are both deeply known."[2] In other words, there is no deep knowing of God without a deep knowing of self, and no deep knowing of self without a deep knowing of God. "Nearly the whole of sacred doctrine," wrote John Calvin, "consists in these two parts: knowledge of God and ourselves."[3]

While there's never been any serious theological dispute with this ancient Christian understanding, it's been largely forgotten or ignored by the contemporary church. While we have focused on knowing God, we've tended to overlook the importance of understanding ourselves. The consequences have been harsh and dramatic. Blind spots abound, resulting in betrayed marriages, decimated families, shipwrecked ministries, and endless numbers of people ruined.

Leaving our self out of the equation can only result in a spirituality that isn't well grounded in experience. Thus it's not rooted in reality. Focusing on knowing God while failing to understand ourselves may produce a good appearance, but it will always leave a gap between appearance and reality.

I was traveling east on I-40 toward my hometown on October 25, 1999, when I heard news of the tragic death of professional golfer Payne Stewart and a group of his friends. Departing central Florida, the jet they were in had flown a ghostly journey halfway across the country, its windows iced over and its occupants incapacitated, before spiraling nose-first into a grassy field. Had I seen the sleek, stylish plane flying overhead that day, I would have been unaware that something was tragically wrong on the inside of that powerful aircraft.

This tragic image serves well as a metaphor for my life nearly thirty years ago. To the casual onlooker, my life looked quite good. I was flying high. My work among high school students was highly praised. And it wasn't all for show. It was clear that God was working; people's lives were changing. But something was wrong inside me. My life—like the Learjet on autopilot—had become a ghostly journey as I maintained a dangerous course with an incapacitated soul. My life was out of control, but I didn't have a clue about the reasons why. Although I had lots of knowledge about the life of Jesus, I didn't know what it meant to be his friend. I had confidence in my ability to do the work of God, but I was clueless when it came to letting God work in me. In my deepest parts, I knew that God was everywhere, but I often wondered and even doubted whether God was in me.

While that season in my life is now a distant memory, it hasn't been forgotten. Since then I've been gradually and continually discovering how to live *with* God instead of *for* God. It has required a lot of painful, necessary discoveries, mostly having to do with blind spots. Consequently, the gap between my public self and my inner self is continually closing, moving me closer to living a more authentic life.

Revelation to Revolution

The revelation that knowing God and myself are interdependent and essential has produced a revolution in my life. It's helped me to understand that neither can proceed very far without the other. Now I know that God loves me in a profoundly personal and experiential way, just as I know my wife loves me; not because she says so, but because I have experienced it.

Attempting to gain self-knowledge apart from knowing our identity in relationship to God quickly leads to self-inflation and self-preoccupation.

On the other hand, having objective knowledge about God is no more transformational than having knowledge about love. The knowledge that transforms is always personal and relational. There's a world of difference between *knowing of* and *knowing about*. People who resist looking deeply at themselves will equally resist looking deeply at God. Both God and self are most fully known in deep, personal relationship to each other.

Peter's Transformational Knowing

A radical change was set in motion on the day that Peter began to follow Jesus. His experience of knowing both God and himself resulted in a fundamental, continual change for the remainder of his life. Just like you and me, Peter had lots of blind spots. As David Benner points out, "The rock on which Christ promised to build his church was remarkably crumbly."[4] However, none of the disciples demonstrated a more profound transformation in their understanding of themselves and God during their three years with Jesus.

Andrew, Peter's brother and business partner, met Jesus first, right away accepting the invitation to follow him. Andrew then went to Peter, told him that he'd found the Messiah, and brought Peter to Jesus so that he could see for himself. Peter's response was the same as his brother's. He immediately left his fishing enterprise to follow Jesus (Matthew 4:18–22). From this account, it's safe to assume that Peter believed that Jesus was the Messiah.

So, what might we safely assume Peter knew then about himself? Our best guesses are only speculative, of course, but if asked, "Who are you?" on the day he dropped his nets and followed Jesus along the shore, Peter would probably have said he was a fisherman. Pressed for more information, he might add, "I can be a bit hot-headed and impulsive." He might even say with a chuckle, "My brother tells me, 'I'm a Ready! Fire! Aim!' kind of guy." It's even conceivable that, as a Jew living in a Roman-occupied world, he might express his longing for a Savior for his people and himself. However, during this stage in his life, it's highly likely that his fears and the extent of his over-confident pride were blind spots.

When I look back on my journey with Jesus, I'm fascinated at how much I thought I knew about God and myself when I was younger. After nearly fifty years of following Jesus, I now recognize that I'm unfinished, incomplete, imperfect, and I have a long way to go. But I'm confident that God is neither surprised nor disappointed by my need for further development. God's work in me will never be finished until I meet Jesus face to face.

Looking ahead to Peter's dramatic encounter with Jesus walking on water (Matthew 14:22–33), it seems reasonable to assume that Peter's belief that Jesus was the Christ would be much firmer and more secure by then. At that point Peter had seen and heard some astonishing things: water turned into wine; teaching like nothing he'd ever heard; lepers, paralytics, and his mother-in-law healed. Beyond these public demonstrations of authority and compassion, he'd observed Jesus during private moments. He'd experienced his warmth, kindness, and the love that flowed from him.

But on this night on the stormy sea, Peter was focused on his survival. If you looked into Peter's eyes that night, there isn't a trace of his usual self-confidence. If you searched his face, you wouldn't find courage. Later on, you will. But on this night, you would see the toxic, heart-racing fear of a man trapped in a killer storm with no way out. He'd been in these kinds of storms before. He knew that they could kill, and he wanted out!

For hours he had desperately pulled on sails, wrestled with oars, searched for hope. He was soaked, bone-tired, and afraid. Seeing Jesus walking on the water only added to his terror.

"Don't be afraid," Jesus said. "Take courage. I am here!" (Matthew 14:27). Were Jesus's words intended to calm their fears? If so, he could have been more explicit than merely saying, "I am here," without giving his name. Do you think this was a strategic "teachable moment"? I don't know, but I suspect so.

Voices and Words

"My sheep listen to my voice," Jesus said. "I know them, and they follow me" (John 10:27). It's curiously striking that Jesus didn't say, "My sheep listen to my *words.*" Our voice and our words are different, aren't they?

Our voice is one of the most personal things about us. You are the only one in all of creation who has *your* voice.

God's voice, too, is intensely personal; it comes from the depths of who God is. There is no other voice like God's. How do you imagine it sounding? I believe that it is kind and gentle, yet indescribably strong.

His *words,* on the other hand, are another matter. Isn't it fascinating that anyone can speak God's words? Even our most despised Enemy can. But they can only speak them with their own voice. Remember how the Enemy spoke God's words to Jesus in the desert? Jesus wisely said, "People do not live by bread alone, but by every word that comes from the mouth of God" (Matthew 4:4). Only God's kind and gentle words, coming from God's mouth, sustain us. They don't when they come from the mouth of a vile and despicable deceiver.

A few weeks ago, our first grandchild was born. Watching Collins recognize her mother and father's voices is a beautiful experience. Soon, Collins will start cooing and singing back to them. It's a sweet and tender intimacy that cannot be expressed with words.

Collins is already learning that she can trust Will and Katie's voices beyond all others. There's a deep attachment forming as Collins continues listening to her parents' voices. Will and Katie are also learning to distinguish Collins's crying and cooing from other infants.

I can't help wondering, rather than being coy or evasive, if Jesus was ascertaining whether his terrified friends recognized his voice and associated it with their safety? The essential question for us is, "How do you and I cultivate familiarity with God's voice?"

We'll never learn to recognize God's voice if we don't have a profound desire to listen and to hear. And following our desire, we must: Practice. Practice. Practice. We also have to learn to be still and quiet, followed by more: Practice. Practice. Practice. Learning to listen, to be still and quiet are enormous challenges in such a noisy, busy, and hurried world. Yet it is essential.

Still Learning

Having heard Jesus's words and perhaps recognizing his voice, Peter immediately responded, "Lord, if it's you, tell me to come to you, walking on water."

No one knows whether it was Peter's faith or his fear that propelled him. Regardless, he wasted no time climbing out of the boat (see Matthew 14:22–33). Everything went well until Peter lost his focus on Jesus and began to sink. Since it doesn't take long for water to rise from your toes to your teeth, Peter's prayer was the shortest he'd ever prayed. Just three words: "Lord, save me!" is all he managed to say.

Jesus's intervention is precisely and perfectly timed. Once again, recognizing the teachable moment, Jesus asked Peter, "Why did you doubt me?" Not: "What's wrong with you?"

Asked about his experience of God after this event, perhaps Peter would say, "God answers prayer! I was afraid I was going to die!" It also seems likely that Peter would enthusiastically express confidence that Jesus must be the Messiah.

If asked what he learned about himself, he might admit to having some blind spots. I imagine him saying, "I never knew I could be so afraid!" He might admit, "Being a fisherman, I always prided myself in my sailing prowess. I reckon I was blind to how afraid and arrogant I can be."

Another blind spot is uncovered when Jesus washes the disciples' feet (John 13). On the heels of Peter's initial and abrupt refusal came Jesus's prediction of Peter's betrayal. Shocked and dismayed by Jesus's prediction, Peter may have wondered, "How could Jesus have such a blind spot and fail to see the reliability of my love and courage?" For Peter, doubting Jesus seemed more reasonable than doubting himself. Peter was still blind to the enormity of his pride and fear.

I shudder to think of the countless times I've challenged God's wisdom and doubted God's goodness. At times I've felt my life was like a revolving door, with pride and fear moving in and out of my life, wreaking havoc with my soul.

After his denial (John 18:15–27), it's likely that Peter was consumed with anguish and remorse. He must have agonized about what he hadn't been able to see: his lack of courage, treasonous disloyalty, and gripping fear. Finally, what can we imagine Peter saying about God and himself after his encounter with the resurrected Jesus? (John 21:15–25).

After returning to his life as a fisherman and spending a night catching nothing, an unrecognizable person on the shore asks about their catch and encourages them to cast their nets on the other side of the boat. When the nets fill with fish, the men recognize that it's Jesus, and Peter leaps overboard, frantically swimming to shore.

Mirroring the pattern of his denials while standing by the fire (remember where Peter was standing when he denied Jesus?), Jesus asks him three times if he loves him more than the other disciples, giving Peter three chances to reaffirm his love.

What would Peter tell us now about his knowledge of God and himself? I'm sure that one thing he'd emphasize is the need for Christ followers to be alert to blind spots. If anyone in the early church knew how easily we can be deceived, it was Peter. When he began walking and working with Jesus, watching how he did life, Peter's blind spots prevented him from seeing his pride and fear. Thus, he was overconfident when danger was near, ignoring Jesus's warnings. He hurried ahead when he should have waited, slept when he should have prayed, and talked when he should have listened. Peter was a courageous but careless Christ follower.

Are You Jesus's Disciple?

I firmly believe that genuine transformation into the character of Christ is possible. It requires learning how to live as disciples of Jesus in our ordinary, everyday lives; in our family, at work, at school, and at play. Ultimately, it all comes down to this: we must allow our initial introduction to Jesus to deepen into a deep, personal knowledge of him and ourselves.

A disciple is someone who studies, learns, and practices the values, priorities, and virtues of the person they are devoted to following. Far more fundamentally and profoundly, a disciple is someone who loves a particular Someone—Someone who wants even more than a close personal relationship with us. The wild, raging, consuming love of God deliberately intends to draw us into a oneness so substantive that once we wake up to it, we realize, "It is no longer I who live, but Christ who lives in me" (Galatians 2:20 ESV).

Following Jesus is the most significant opportunity and highest privilege ever afforded you and me. Despite the undeniable difficulty and complexity involved, our heart's desire for real-life—life as God intended—will never be satisfied until that desire transcends all of the questions, insecurities, and concerns that accompany the decision to be an disciple.

Perhaps some self-disclosure will help bring what I mean into focus. When my wife and I married, truthfully, I had a lot of fundamental unanswered questions: Can we afford to be married? Are we mature enough? Will we regret the decision? My longing to experience a lifetime of oneness with her trumped all of my concerns. Following Jesus into a lifetime of oneness is like that, but on a much grander, eternal scale. Our destination, safety, or survival are not the primary issue. The focus, goal, and reward lie in *following Jesus*. Thus, the essence of what it means to be an disciple is simply living in the reality of our oneness with God.

After three years of doing life together, Peter must have found Jesus's departure into heaven a huge adjustment. It forced him to learn new ways of keeping company with him and letting him inhabit every dimension of his life. Peter's aim became the ongoing transformation of his spiritual core—the place of thought and feeling, will and character. For followers of Jesus ever since, there has been a vital link between the desire for real life, keeping company with Jesus who lives within, and devotion to spiritual practices and habits.

Training, Not Trying

Being a disciple is less about "trying" and more about "training" as we begin living into the reality of God living within us. Therefore, the point of spiritual practices and habits is not to strive for something we don't yet have but rather to enjoy the gift we've already been given.

If this is true, then our motivation, approach, and practice of spiritual practices shift dramatically. Instead of striving to get closer to God or earn God's approval and affection, we're free to enjoy these gifts. This helps us understand that our habits and routines involving prayer, Bible reading and study, service to others, and doing life together with others are like points on a map, leading to a priceless treasure. They are not the treasure itself, merely the way we get there.

We must devote ourselves to these practices. However, we miss an essential point and endanger our souls whenever we think of spiritual practices as ends in themselves. We maintain them to create space in our lives for a heightened awareness of God's always-and-forever presence in our life. They are never the be-all and end-all of discipleship. Ultimately, following Jesus is about cultivating a loving trust of—and submission to—the God who is both within us and beyond our very best efforts.

As essential as they are, spiritual practices must never become a *substitute* for following Jesus and living in oneness with God. We are susceptible to making this mistake because the self-absorbed quest to be in control of our well-being is the natural energy in every human soul. Whenever we yield to that desire, our spiritual practices lose some of their purpose and power. Thus, practicing various spiritual habits is like a person "working on their tan." The "work" is mostly about positioning ourselves so that God can do what only God can do—transform us into the likeness of Jesus. This is why some speak of spiritual practices as "the path of disciplined grace." Everything is a gift. Prayer, Scripture reading, solitude, silence—these are *graces* because they are freely given to us. They are *disciplines* because there is something we can and must do. And that something has more to do with positioning than striving, more to do with conformity to Jesus's values and way of living than our huffing and puffing to become like him.

The life God uniquely designed for us to live and for which our hearts yearn cannot be achieved by our efforts, no matter how disciplined we may be or how hard we try. Instead, it comes only by way of a few prepositions: *with, in,* and *for*—what pastor and author Eugene Peterson call "prepositional participation." These prepositions join us to God and God's activity in our life. They are the essential ways and means of being in on what God intends to accomplish.

Be Encouraged

One of the most significant realizations of my life is the mysterious, liberating reality of my oneness with God, who unconditionally loves and accepts me as I am because of what Christ has done for me. Though I am far from perfect, with blind spots yet to be revealed, I'm nonetheless dazzled by the diminishing of my restless striving to earn God's approval and to grow closer to the One who *already* is closer than close. Instead, my life is being gradually and radically renovated, from the inside out, by the One who lives within.

Get Engaged

I hope you know by now that you have blind spots and that what you don't see can hurt you. If you're not convinced, I dare you to ask someone who knows you well to tell you what they think. I believe we all have blind spots because we all struggle with sin. I know I do, and I have my wife's confirmation.

From the beginning of this book, Tim and I have tried to offer some things you can do about them.

Here's a final suggestion. Psalm 19:1–11 is a prayer celebrating God's glory in creation and the law. Then, abruptly, the psalmist David asks God a question followed by a plea:

"How can I know all the sins lurking in my heart? Cleanse me from these hidden faults" (Psalm 19:12). Friend, you and I can be as openly transparent with God as we're able and yet we still have blind spots. The psalmist did too. So, we invite you to consider a challenge. Every day for the next thirty days, pray this prayer: *"How can I know all the sins lurking in my heart? Cleanse me from these hidden faults."*

Who knows, you might discover yourself living with fewer blind spots.

Endnotes

Chapter 1

1. John Calvin, *Institutes of the Christian Religion*, quoted by Alice Fryling in *Mirror for the Soul: A Christian Guide to the Enneagram* (Downers Grove, IL: InterVarsity Press, 2017), 19.

2. David Benner, "Brokenness and Wholeness," Dr. David G. Benner (blog), June 3, 2016, www.drdavidg benner.ca/brokenness-and-wholeness.

Chapter 2

1. "Dunning-Kruger Effect," Wikipedia, https:// en.wikipedia.org/wiki/Dunning–Kruger_effect.

2. "Imposter Syndrome," Wikipedia, https://en.wiki pedia.org/wiki/Impostor_syndrome.

Chapter 3

1. Travis Meadows, "Sideways," *First Cigarette*, McDowell Road Records, under exclusive license to Blaster Records, LTD, October 13, 2017. Used by permission.

Chapter 4

1. "The Titanic: Lifeboats," History on the Net, https://www.historyonthenet.com/the-titanic-lifeboats.

Chapter 5

1. Footnote to John 9:2 in *The NIV Study Bible* (Grand Rapids: Zondervan Publishing House, 1985), 1614.

2. Philip Yancey, *The Jesus I Never Knew* (Grand Rapids: Zondervan Publishing House, 1995), 169–70.

3. Ruth Harms Calkin; this paraphrase of Romans 8:38–39 appeared in a sermon by Ray Stedman, the long-time pastor of Peninsula Bible Church in Palo Alto, California and author of several books. Ray Stedman, "If God Be for Us," Series: From Guilt to Glory, https://www.raystedman.org/new-testament/romans/if-god-be-for-us.

Chapter 6

1. Michael Yaconelli, *Messy Spirituality: God's Annoying Love for Imperfect People* (Grand Rapids: Zondervan, 2002), 16.

2. Henri Nouwen, "Care, the Source of All Cure," http://henrinouwen.org/meditation/care-the-source-of-all-cure/.

Chapter 9

1. Thomas Merton, *Thoughts in Solitude* (Boston: Shambhala, 1993), 55.

2. David Benner, *The Gift of Being Yourself* (Downers Grove, IL: InterVarsity Press, 2004), 20.

3. John Calvin, *Institutes of the Christian Religion*, 1536 ed., trans. Ford Lewis Battles (Grand Rapids: Eerdmans, 1995), 15.

4. Benner, *The Gift of Being Yourself*, 26.